I Did It Afraid

He Was There All the Time

Cheryl Ann Masaitis-Spychaj

He Was There All the Time

In memory of my deceased husband, Greg, who strongly encouraged me to write my life story because he felt it would bless and help others in their own faith journey.

In honor of my beloved husband, Marvin, who also said you have a story to share and you must "write it."

Many names and places have been withheld for reasons of privacy and confidentiality. Biblical references in this book are taken from the New American Bible, Catholic Edition of the Revised Version.

Copyright November 13, 2017

Printed in the United States of America

All rights reserved

ISBN-13:
978-1979759502

ISBN-10:
1979759502

spychaj.publishing@yahoo.com

This book is available through Amazon.com

Contents

Introduction 5
Beginnings 9
High School 25
A Step Back, Walking Down Memory Lane 37
College & Beyond 43
Teaching Years 57
FBI Days 73
NYC, Gotham, the Big Apple 93
Marriage, Bible School & Family 113
Preparing for the Mission Field 131
What Next, Lord? 143
Walking by Faith 159
The Move to Missouri 167
A New Adventure Begins 181
Home Again in the Heartland 199
Post Mortem 211
I'm Coming Home, Mom 235
A New Beginning 247
A New Life 261
Reflections of My Journey With the Lord 271
Growing in Wholeness and Grace 295
Epilogue 309

He Was There All the Time

Introduction

The story I am sharing with you is a beautiful love story. It's His story, my story but truly "our story." It is a love story between my beloved Lord and me. Through all the crazy twists and turns of my life, He has been there all the time. Listening to His still, small voice and following Him has not always been an easy task. In fact, sometimes I have gone way out on the limb, but He has never left me there. God has continually called me back to a deeper more intimate relationship with Himself. Exodus 34:14 says: "You shall not bow down to any other god, for the Lord-Jealous- His name-is a jealous God!" And I am so glad He is. So often I have been afraid of what He is going to ask of me and I have run away or run to lesser "gods" that don't fulfill the deep calling within my heart; however, when He does call me back, with His help, I have so often just plain "done it afraid." I have not waited until all the fear and doubt have vanished. It rarely ever does go away. I have just said, "OK Lord, let's just go forward and do what you are asking me to do when nothing makes sense to me." Not knowing where we will go or what we will do, like a

He Was There All the Time

little child, I just hold His hand and say, "Daddy God, where would you have us go today and what would you have us to do? Thy will, not mine be done." Easier said than done! This truly has been a great adventure of love as I learn to let go of control and trust His will, His way, His means and His timing in all the events and circumstances of my life. Simply put: just get out of the boat and walk on water with Him.

Life is a journey full of many twists and turns for all of us, and my life is no different. A counselor once told me God writes straight with crooked lines and that is truly the story of my life. From the time of my youth, I used to love to read about other people's life journeys. Their stories of heroic adventure fascinated me. But I never thought of writing my own story until several people (from all backgrounds who have heard bits and pieces of my life story) have strongly encouraged me to write. They have wanted to hear the whole story from my childhood until now. What is so beautiful is that we all have a unique and amazing life story. I am learning as I get older, that we are very needy people. Not only do we need a personal relationship with the living God, but we also need each other. God did not make us to be lone rangers. We all have something to share so as to help, encourage and strengthen each other as we journey through this life on our way home to heaven. If in any way my story will help someone else on their journey it will have been worth the cost of sharing and exposing my heart in all its brokenness and healing.

For years, I had held back writing because I was so ashamed of what I have done and been through. Pride, the root of all evil, has held me back from being vulnerable, transparent and honest. I have not wanted to hurt anyone -- especially my family. In sharing my story, I need to share my perceptions of what I felt it was like growing up in a very loving yet wounded family. It has not been an easy journey and it has taken me a long time to accept God's unconditional love and merciful forgiveness. I am now beginning to realize that I have not needed to "earn His love" but that He loves me no matter what I have been through.

My life journey has been a slow process of learning the truth, of being healed and set free. I see life so differently now than I did years ago. I now see that we are all born sinners, but that God loves us and is calling each of us to be saints who daily live in His light, love and presence. I also see the Catholic Church as a home, a safe-haven from the storms of life as well as a hospital where we can be healed. It is anchored in Jesus Christ who is the way, truth and life (See John 14:6). In this home, we have a Father (Abba, PaPa, Daddy God), Jesus, (our Lord and Savior and beloved husband to us His bride), the Holy Spirit who unites us to Jesus and the Father in the love they share, and Our Blessed Mother who is not only Jesus' mother but our mother too. They

He Was There All the Time

are all rooting for us to know their love and mercy in a personal and deep way and to see us get safely to heaven.

I am writing my story in a conversational style -- as if I was sitting down and sharing my life journey with a good friend. I write the way I speak. I simply want to share from my heart who God is and what He has done and continues to do in my life. I know myself to be a selfish, prideful sinner and I have come to know my God as a loving Father full of mercy for His lost child.

Beginnings

My father was an only child born out of wedlock to a teenage mother who was unable to care for him. As a child, I loved to listen to my Dad tell stories of his life growing up, even though it was not a pretty picture. Sometimes I would want to cry when I heard them. Instead of being angry or depressed over the terrible things that happened to him as a child, he chose to turn to God and trust Him with his life. To give you a little background, back in the mid-1920's you would be shamed for having a child outside of marriage. My dad grew up thinking that his grandmother was his real mother and that his real mother was his sister. What a horrible day it was for him, at the tender age of twelve, to hear the devastating news that his "sister" was his real mother and that she had to move away from home to seek a job in another city. To make matters worse, dad's "grandma" was getting too old to care for him so they sent him to Canada to live with his father who by then had gotten married. During his short time on the family farm,

He Was There All the Time

his father told my dad that he was never to tell anyone that he was his son. He was to tell everyone that he was "a hired hand". His wife felt sorry for the boy, so she asked her husband to at least let him stay in their house and have meals with them, which he agreed to; however, he continued to mistreat my dad in other ways. For example, when the weather got bad and it was too cold and snowy to ride his bike to school, his dad would attach his bike to his truck and pull him along. I recall dad telling me how he would fly off his bike when his dad would drive too fast. Due to these horrific circumstances, my dad did not last there very long and begged to come back to the states; however, he had no home to go back to and like Jesus, no place to rest his head (See Matthew 8:20).

Upon his return to the states, he connected with an old schoolmate and asked him if he could live with him and his parents. They were a very poor family and the dad was blind. The mother said she could not see them bringing another child into their home when they barely had enough for themselves; however, the father said that this child was homeless and how could they turn him away. My dad learned many wonderful lessons from this blind man who could really see with the heart of God beyond circumstances. They never went without. My dad learned about real love from this blind man.

To give you an idea what an incredible man my dad was, while I was growing up, every summer, my dad would call his father and ask if we could come visit him in Canada and take him and his wife out to dinner. Sometimes they came "south" to visit us and we would always have a great time with them. When his father died, dad made sure that we all went up to Canada to the funeral home to pay our respects to our grandfather. Then, he went a step further and offered to help his dad's widow in any way she needed, asking nothing in return. He was truly a man of God, knowing that nothing would be left to him, the only son, of his father's wealthy estate after his widow died. But dad honored God by doing the right thing for his father and stepmother.

At the age of 18, dad left this wonderful blind man's family to begin a life of his own by joining the army. His dream was to be a pilot, but due to a shoulder injury, he could not fulfill his heart's desire; however, he was still able to serve as a crewman and fly with the other soldiers on missions. I recall a powerful story that dad told me as a child. He said that many people think that Friday the 13th is an unlucky day, a day to be feared but not him! One Friday the 13th, while doing practice flights, the pilot asked that one man stay off the plane. There were twelve men plus the pilot. He told the soldiers that he never flew with thirteen people on his plane on Friday the 13th; however, no one wanted to stay back. The pilot was forced to select one person and he chose my father. Although very disappointed, my father stayed back. Shortly after takeoff the plane crashed, and all twelve men aboard were killed. After that my Dad always referred to Friday the 13th as his lucky day! I too was blessed many years later, on Friday the 13th as well.

After fulfilling his military commitment, dad chose to leave the army and returned home to make a life for himself as a civilian. He loved talking to people and was very friendly.   He also was easily approachable and very warm hearted to anyone and everyone! Not knowing what to do with his life, he decided to become a salesman. His humble beginnings were to sell jewelry door to door. In a short time, he became quite successful and opened his own jewelry store. During those early years he decided to start attending daily Mass. He found great strength in receiving the Lord in Eucharist each day and the Lord mercifully looked after him. In fact, his name means beloved of God. Shortly thereafter, he met a lovely lady and they started dating.

 Mom came from a "very different side of the track", as she would put it. She grew up with very strict Italian parents who had come to the states by boat from Sicily prior to her birth. She was the youngest of four living children and very spoiled by her parents. Her siblings were much older than her, so she felt like an only child growing up. Her dad was a shoemaker but got very sick and had to quit work when she was a teenager. At that point, her papa stayed home and took care of his precious little daughter while mama went back to work. But he died when she was about 16 years old, leaving her very broken-hearted inside. She adored her dad and I believe that the void was not filled until she met my dad. Grandma was very protective of her daughter and only wanted the best for her. Although dad's background was not the greatest, Grandma loved his warm and caring ways and gave her blessing for their marriage.

Soon after they were married, dad had a lovely home built for his bride and a new life began. Mom helped in the jewelry store and life was good. Financially, they were prospering and spiritually they were growing in their Catholic faith together as husband and wife. Dad continued to go to daily Mass and together they always went to Sunday Mass. They loved all the Catholic traditions and kept them faithfully. At Christmas time, Dad would go out looking for the biggest, bushiest tree he could find and surprise my mom with his findings. The tree would always take over the living room, but they had fun decorating every inch of it! More importantly, they rejoiced over the real meaning of Christmas: the birth of our Lord.

Soon after marriage, they desired to have a family. But the first two pregnancies resulted in one still born and one miscarriage. Being a very anxious person who worried about everything, mom relied heavily on our Lord and His Mother for strength, after such devastating losses. When she became pregnant with me, she prayed that I would be born healthy and on time. She later told me that two months prior to my birth, she knelt before baby Jesus in the manger under the Christmas tree and asked Him to keep me safe and healthy until I was born. I believe that my mom's prayers that day and the many times afterwards, have saved and rescued me through the dangers and losses in my life. As a mother, I now know that God hears and answers a Mother's prayers for her beloved children. May we never stop praying for them!

The Lord heard the cry of this precious Mother's heart and brought me safely into the world one cold, wintery February day in 1953; however, I was born weighing about 5 lbs. or a little less and had to be kept in the hospital until I gained more weight. It was another blow to my Mother as she continued to pray and visit me each day. But with God's help and wonderful medical care, I gained weight and was then able to come home into her arms of tender love.

Quickly our little family grew from one to five siblings -- with another miscarriage in between -- and it was time to move out of our little house into a big bungalow that could accommodate all of us. Being the eldest child, I always felt responsible for my younger brother and sisters; however, I was not always the best example. I remember one time when, as a little girl, I got into trouble for putting my younger sister in the dryer. In trying to get out, she broke the glass door and boy, was I in trouble! I realized at a very young age how self-centered, selfish and sinful I was. Another time, I convinced my brother to smash a cake that was sitting on our neighbor's front porch. Then I tried to deny my part in this mean act. As a little girl, I wondered why I was so mean. I had little understanding of sin at the time. As the Bible says: We are born with original sin in us (See Romans 3:23). Another time I recall riding my bike on the sidewalk and a huge dog was in my way. I yelled to him to get out of the way, but he just stayed there so I ran right into him. Unfortunately, I was the one who suffered the consequences of my mean act when I flew off my bike and hit the concrete real hard and cracked off part of my front tooth! I felt so ashamed that I never wanted to get it fixed despite several attempts on my parent's part to get the tooth repaired. I felt I deserved this punishment to remind me of my selfish, sinful ways. As my Dad would oftentimes say: "You made your bed, now you lie in it."

I do recall another story that left a profound effect, on my mind as a little child. My brother had been very sick and almost died when he was about two years old. In fact, a priest came to the hospital to administer him the last rites – Extreme Unction as it was called back then -- but my mom took a firm stand of faith and said "No! He will not die, but live!" She could not bear the thought of losing yet another child! She went down to the chapel in the hospital and cried out to the Lord for her little boy to live. While crying, a heavy set, elderly nun came up to her and asked what was wrong. She

He Was There All the Time

told the sister that her baby boy was dying, and the nun told her to say this prayer: "Lord, he whom thou lovest, is sick." (Years later my mom learned that this was a verse from the Bible; (see John 11:3). When Mom looked up from her tears she discovered that the nun had disappeared. She prayed the prayer and immediately ran to her son's bedside. Shortly thereafter, he did have a miraculous recovery and mom wanted to thank this sweet nun for praying with her. When she asked the nurses who this nun was, they said they had never seen anyone who fit the description that mom gave. Mom believed then it must have been an angel sent by God at the time she needed the comfort and strength the most. Around this same time, I became real sick and after trying various remedies nothing was working. Mom and dad decided to take all of us on a train ride up to Chicago to St. Jude's shrine. We were all prayed over and returned home. Soon after, the doctor found a cure for me simply by looking up my condition in his medical book! Another miracle and answer to a mother's cry for help.

When I was about 7 or 8 years old, I started to notice that mom would be very sad at times. I recall one day an incident where I felt very alone and abandoned. We were playing outside in front of our house. I was steering my little red wagon on the uneven sidewalk while, at my request, my sister pushed me real fast. When I hit an uneven crack I flipped over, fell out and blood covered my face. Immediately I ran up the driveway only to find the back door locked! I could not believe mom had locked us out. I started screaming for her and it seemed an eternity before she heard me. Then she yelled out of an upper room window in an annoyed way asking what I wanted. I felt so ashamed that I had upset her so much that day. I think she had been napping. I sensed something was wrong with mom, but I was just a child and I did not know.

When I was about 9 years old, we moved into our big beautiful home that Dad and Mom had custom built. It was their dream home, complete with an in- ground swimming pool, which they had put in a few years later. Although we were all excited about this move, mom was not. Around this time, she had her fifth child and subsequently fell into severe depression which eventually culminated in a total mental breakdown. It was a very painful experience to visit mom in a mental institution and not understand how or why all this happened. My precious mama became a different person after receiving shock treatments. I did not recognize her, and she could barely recognize us. I was so scared that we were going to lose her.

Strangely enough, I recall desiring to feel close to Jesus during this time in my life. I remember being in my bedroom one day and saying to the Lord: "I wish I could have been Mary who had given birth to Him. I wanted Jesus to live in my heart so bad so that I could mother Him too." Little did I know that He would answer this

He Was There All the Time

little girl's heart prayer, many years later, but in a way, I never expected. I just wanted to be so close to Jesus and have Him live inside me the way he lived in Mary. I also wanted and needed a mom, like Mary, who I could feel close to because my mom seemed so very far from me, emotionally.

Mom finally came home after a very long hospital stay but she was not the same person I knew before she had her breakdown. We would come home from school and each day we would find her curled up in a chair resting in our dark family room. I always was hoping that we could tell her about our day's events; instead, we would hear her yell, "take off your clothes and go do your homework." Not the kind of welcome I longed for. This went on for quite some time. Living with a very depressed mom who was so negative and critical about everything left a devastating effect on my young impressionable life. I found my solace in going to morning Mass and spending quality time with my dad each Saturday.

Unfortunately, at the young age of ten to twelve, I saw myself getting very depressed as well. Dad had major problems with his business in addition to Mom's health problems, so I became his sounding board. After Saturday Mass, we would go out for breakfast and have very long talks. Because he had no one to confide in, he would pour out all his serious problems to me. He would talk, and I would listen and take to heart the things he shared with me. I felt like it was my responsibility to bring some joy and happiness into my dad's life because I believed my mom was unable to do so. I never wanted to add to his burdens, so I never told him how I felt about anything with which I was dealing. I chose to close my heart real tight so that I could support and love and care for him and not put any more pressure on him than he already felt. I simply smiled on the outside and listened to him pour out all his problems to me while holding all my pain and concerns inside; however, my little heart could not handle all this pressure at such a tender young age. On one occasion, I recall my dad telling me a terrible story about my mom. He met with her doctor who said that he should divorce her because she was unfit for him and could not fulfill his needs as a wife. My dad told the doctor he would never do such a thing because of his love for God and his strong Catholic faith. In childlike immaturity, I really thought our family was falling apart and that we might lose everything and end up living under a bridge!

At this same time, I remember going to confession and telling the priest that I wanted to die, and he said that we need to have a talk as soon as possible. I was scared to tell my dad that this priest needed to talk to me in his office. I feared my dad pressuring me to tell him why I had to keep this urgent appointment, but he didn't ask, and I didn't tell. Instead, he simply took me to see this kind priest who put the fear of God in me. He told me that if I ever

He Was There All the Time

decided to do something to myself, I could end up in hell and that was not the answer to my family's problems. He made me promise not to hurt myself and, if I kept my promise, he would not tell my parents why I came to see him. He put such fear into me that I never acted upon those feelings at the time. But I recall feeling that it was my fault that dad was having financial problems at work and that mom was so sick.

Although I was always concerned about my dad's welfare, I did a very foolish thing in the 5th grade. I lied on a hearing test that they gave us in school. I said I could not hear all the beeps, so they told my parents I needed to see a specialist. I never dreamed that my little joke would end up like this! I felt awful, thinking I had just placed a worse burden on my dad. Fortunately, the test results came back normal, but I still felt awful for creating such a ruckus for my parents.

One day, while in 6th grade, I realized I could no longer see the board at school (for real- no joke this time!) so I was given an eye test and was told I needed glasses. I was so shaken up over this, because of the grief I had caused my parents the year before. I hid the prescription thinking I can't put another financial burden on my dad. I really thought that this burden would put him over the edge and I wanted to spare him. But the problem only got worse. One day out of fear and trepidation, thinking I might go blind, I told my dad that I needed to see an eye doctor and get glasses. I remember telling him how awful I felt that I had to put this burden on him on top of all the other burdens he was carrying. He laughed and said it was nothing to worry about. I felt so relieved to know that he was not upset with me and quickly, thereafter, I got my first pair of glasses.

During these vulnerable years, I struggled to please my parents in the hopes of making them happy and to bring some brightness into their life. I felt this was my responsibility and I wanted desperately to be a blessing and not another burden.

When we moved into our new home, my father asked my mom's older sister, a widow, to come live with us. My aunt became like a second mother to us five kids and a great right hand to my dad who was trying to run a business and care for us, during Mom's illness and recuperation. As time went on, it was decided that it was in Mom's best interest for her to join my Dad at his business. This seemed to be a good fit for her mental and emotional health and well-being.

During this transition, I continued to struggle in many ways unbeknown to my parents. I thought the only way to feel good about myself and to bring happiness to them was to be an excellent student and try to get all A's. I worked very hard at being a top student, but in my Catholic school they classified students by ability level. I always ended up in the "B" classroom and that

He Was There All the Time

hurt my pride and self-image. Most of my friends were in the "A" classroom which made me feel so inferior to them. As hard as I tried, I never made it into the "A" classroom and always felt I was not good enough so I kept on trying harder and harder to be more perfect. This plan worked because my parents always applauded my good grades. My mom was a perfectionist and I wanted so badly to be perfect in everything I did so that she would love me and hopefully get better. I just wanted to see her happy and not so negative and sad all the time.

When I was about twelve years old, some dreams started emerging in my heart. My parents subscribed to various missionary magazines and I loved reading the stories about overseas missionaries. I began to desire that kind of life; but I also had other conflicting desires. I really wanted to be married, have a large family and adopt special needs children whom no one else would want. I knew if I wanted to be a missionary, I would have to become a nun—after all the only females who were missionaries were nuns -- and being a nun did not interest me at all! For many years, I was deeply torn by these conflicting desires.

One summer, Dad and Mom rented a cottage up in Canada on the beach. We loved jumping the waves and swimming until exhaustion. My parents loved parties and one day they invited a friend over who had a speed boat. He was going to teach us kids how to water ski. How exciting that was to try something new and different. I had never been on skis before and, as hard as I tried, I could not get the hang of it! The man got frustrated with me and decided to jump into the water to show me exactly how it was done. When he jumped in, his very expensive diamond ring fell off his finger and there went my lesson! We were in very deep water and it was nearly impossible to even see the sand below. I felt awful about the situation and blamed myself for this mishap when I saw how very upset he was with me. The truth was, he probably was more upset with himself than me, but I felt responsible for this situation. I knew there was not much I could do but pray real hard that God would do a miracle. The man decided that we should go back to shore very carefully so as not to create waves and call a scuba diver. The challenge was how he would ever explain exactly where the ring fell off when there was nothing around us but deep water! The scuba diver decided it was best to go out the next morning while the water was calm and try searching for a tiny speck in a huge lake. I never prayed so hard in my life. Oh, how I wanted this man to get his diamond ring back but what chance -- barring a miracle -- that the ring would be found. By the next day it probably would have sunk into the sand especially if there were waves during the night. But with child-like faith I cried out to God to please lead the scuba diver to the exact location of that ring and when he came back to shore, there in his hand was the ring! He found it and I learned that day the power of prayer and child-like faith.

He Was There All the Time

I Did It Afraid

High School

When it was time to go to high school, I was accepted into a very good all girls, private, Catholic school, on one condition: summer school for reading and math. Once again, I had to face the realization that I was not very smart. Both reading and math came very hard to me. I could not comprehend or recall what I read very well. Even though my dad was a math wizard, and my mom a very good reader, I did not inherit their "scholastic" genes. If I read something over and over, it would eventually come, but after great struggle. For the most part, school never came easy to me. I simply had to work very hard at all my subjects.

In 9th grade I was placed in the second to the lowest classroom, feeling once again very inferior to all my friends who were in the smarter classes. I could not accept the fact that school was just plain hard for me. The reality of my situation hit me when I found myself failing science class. I went to my teacher, and told her I

He Was There All the Time

just could not understand the concepts she was teaching. Although she was very sick at the time, this young nun, decided to work with me after school for as long as I needed her help. She hid the seriousness of her sickness so well that I did not even know how sick she was until after school was over that summer. By the end of the school year, my grades went from failure to the high 90's all because of a very special person who took time to care and help me succeed. I recall, when they were giving out awards at the end of the school year, I received the award for the most improved, yet I knew in my heart that this was a tribute to this precious nun. Soon after I received the award, I was informed that she had died. Could she have been kept alive just for me? Sister was a gift from God. She gave me hope to carry on, to keep trying harder and to never give up no matter how difficult things got in my life.

I loved singing and acting and wanted so badly to be in school plays. To help with my shyness, I started attending drama school where I took private lessons in public speaking and acting. I even took private voice lessons so that I could try out for the school musicals. One year I wanted to have the lead role in our school play, but I knew my voice was not as strong as the other girl who tried out. Her voice was loud and powerful, but my voice sounded like a church mouse -- quiet and squeaky. Once again, I felt like a failure. I ended up with a tiny role with just a few lines! However, my drama school teacher was a former British actress herself and she saw great potential in me. She encouraged me to keep on acting and told me she could see me as a very good actress someday. But God had other plans.

During my high school years, I also took organ lessons because I loved music as well. When I told my music teacher what my drama teacher had told me, she said the acting and music business are very hard professions to make a living at and that I should just do them as an avocation. She was the realist and again, I was devastated to hear this. Eventually I just gave up my dream of going to Hollywood and becoming a great singer/actress!

When I was about 16 years old, I had a very real encounter with the Lord in the library at school. Out of the blue, I heard a voice in my heart say something to the effect, "Will you give your heart/life to me." I had never had such an experience and it threw me because I somehow knew that it was the Lord speaking to my heart. I really thought He was asking me to be nun and that was the last thing I ever wanted. In my heart, I really wanted to be a missionary but not a nun. I remember also thinking that means I would have to give up my dreams of being a mom, (having several children of my own as well as adopting special needs children) and living a fulfilled married life. As I pondered this dilemma, I started to cry and said "No, Lord, I just can't do this." I believed a lie of Satan who convinced me that God wanted to rob me of my

He Was There All the Time

dreams. That day I ran from God, doubting His goodness and wonderful plans for my life (See Jeremiah 29:11-13). Instead of letting go and letting God decide what was best for me, I opened the door to Satan to use this situation to further hurt me later in my life. I became my own "little god" deciding what I thought was best for my life. By becoming my own "little god", I made my dreams my idols. They were all good dreams, but I was putting my dreams before love of God and asking Him what His dreams were for me. They were more important than God's will and plans for my life. Basically, I became the LORD of my life instead of God and, from that day on, I saw myself as a fugitive running FROM God rather than TO Him with my desires. My fears were two-fold: I feared what I thought He wanted me to become (a nun) and what I thought He wanted me to give up (my dreams). I was not ready to let go of my heartfelt dreams. I felt like God was a dream robber. How sad to think I fell for this lie of Satan which I have since repented.

Another terrible decision I made was to vow that no man was going to tell me what to do. I felt that my Dad was very controlling because he would tell me my dreams were "heavenly bound and earthly worthless" and I needed to be realistic and let go of them. This too caused me emotional issues later in life of which I have since repented.

In my quest for truth and meaning in life, I recall going on a retreat with some classmates to the nuns' summer home – or convent -- in the country. A wonderful priest was our retreat director and I just felt so comfortable talking to him about my search for truth and meaning in life. He was a beautiful, humble, godly man with whom I felt safe. I trusted him to lead me on the right path. But my trust was shattered soon after the retreat was over.

One night the nuns went to sleep early and let us girls stay up unsupervised. I remember one of my friends saying let's levitate each other but I got scared because I had never been exposed to this type of witchcraft before. After not seeing anything happen, I decided to go to bed. The next morning, they bragged on how they succeeded in levitating each other after I left the room. I believe the Lord was watching over me that night! I was confused that such a thing could happen on a retreat. Wasn't this sinful and wrong? I also wondered why the nuns would ever have left us alone so late at night! Why weren't they supervising us more carefully? But this was not the only thing that spiritually disturbed me. I found out, soon after the retreat, that this wonderful priest, whom I adored, and thought was so Godly, had left the priesthood to get married! I was shocked and deeply saddened by this news.

I had grown up thinking that priests and nuns were so very holy and close to God. I was raised to think that they have a higher calling than us lay people, so I saw them as almost perfect and on a pedestal. This was another lie of Satan that hurt me in my search for truth. I was focused on people (nuns and priests or those in spiritual leadership) and their behavior instead of our God who alone is perfect (See Psalm 118:8). It has taken me a long time to see people in ministry as human beings with weaknesses and failings just like me. I see how much our priests need our prayers because without priests we do not have the sacraments which give us the grace to walk with God. Satan wants to taint their reputation and their effect on naïve people like me who trusted them. My eyes were people-centered rather than God-centered. I saw their failures as a failure of the Catholic Church because they represented the Catholic Church to me.

During this time, I also was terribly upset that one of our parish priests, who was a good friend of my parents, left the priesthood to marry one of the nuns who taught in our grammar school! I could not get a grip on all of this. Then to make matters worse, my mom's brother -- who used to come over to our house almost every day -- committed suicide. He too suffered from severe depression like my mom. Before he died, he once told me to be very careful what you do because God sees everything. I knew what that priest years ago had told me about hurting oneself and here he did that very thing himself. What was going through his mind when he took his life? Did he think God was approving his act? Did he believe what he told me that God sees everything we do and judges us according to our deeds? All these situations played havoc on my heart and mind as I was trying to figure out my faith, morality and truth. It appeared everyone was doing what seemed right in their own eyes!

On the upside, my dad used to earn international trips to faraway countries through selling appliances and, on a few of those occasions, he would take us kids with mom and him. I loved my trip to Spain because it was exciting to meet other people from a different culture and learn about their lives. He also took me on a Caribbean cruise. On both trips, I got very sick with severe stomach pain, yet it didn't stop me from enjoying our travels. It just confirmed my desire to live overseas and be a missionary someday despite my very weak, sensitive stomach!

As I wrote earlier, I had a strong desire to be a missionary from about the age of twelve and I tried to read about all kinds of missionaries and their work. I loved reading their stories and thinking about their overseas adventures. One day I read an in-depth article in the newspaper about a diocesan priest who was working among the very poor in Peru. I really wanted to hear about his work firsthand, so I diligently sought out his address from the local newspaper, and wrote to him. He only wrote to me a few times but enough to convince me that this was truly my life's calling. I loved hearing his stories and I just wanted to be where he was and doing the things he was doing. It just all felt so right in my heart but again I would hear Dad's words: "You are so heavenly bound and earthly worthless." After a time, I forgot about my dreams of ever becoming a missionary. BUT GOD saw my heart and did the totally unexpected years later. For God often works in strange, mysterious and very unexpected ways as time would tell.

During my teen years, I had some other emotionally painful experiences happen that left a deep impression on my heart. During my weekly breakfasts with dad, he would tell me about mom's struggle with some very deep and personal problems. This was very upsetting to me, but I also realized he had no one else to share his burden with so I lovingly listened. Based on his open honest talks with me -- which focused on all kinds of issues, including the issue of sexual purity, I began to think that sex was evil and that I should avoid it like the plague. As I reflect on these talks now, I think some of these discussions came from his own fears (of being born out of wedlock and having to struggle to be loved and accepted). I am sure that he wanted to protect his girls from ever having this happen to them. To add to the complexity of this situation, one night at dinner, dad had a stern talk with my sisters and me. He said that "if any of you girls ever come home pregnant, I will throw you out of the house!" I know he didn't mean it the way it came out, however this terrified me because I feared being thrown out of their hearts as well. Not only did I now have a fear of sex, I also had a fear of getting pregnant and being rejected by my parents. Unable to talk to mom or dad freely about these "normal emotions" (regarding my sexuality) that were emerging, I just thought there was something terribly wrong with me. Little did I realize that what I was feeling was normal and healthy for this time in my life.

Despite my fears, I did not know how or whom to talk to about these growing up issues. I really wanted to fulfill this need someday in marriage with a loving husband, but I felt it was wrong to even think such thoughts. Because of these "normal desires," I did not think I could ever be a nun. For this reason, I said no to the Lord in the library. Unfortunately, this unresolved issue came back to haunt me a few years later.

During my high school years when I would I share with my parents my dreams of becoming an overseas missionary, being married, having a large family and adopting special needs kids, I would recall my dad's retort about being "heavenly bound and earthly worthless". Hearing it so often, I began to believe that I was worthless and should not be alive because I was stealing air from those who had a right to be here. This was another lie of Satan that I believed. Mom would tell me I was so idealistic and very naïve, and I was! But I could not get rid of those passionate dreams. They only intensified as time went by. My parents used to compare me to my siblings and tell them how obedient and

He Was There All the Time

perfect I was. (Little did they know the internal struggles I was battling!) It was a horrible place to be but to win their approval I worked all the harder to be a people-pleaser just to gain their love. The other kids were always being told how imperfect they were compared to goody-two shoes, Cheryl. I hated it because it was an impossible standard to live up to, but I had to try to act perfect, so that I would feel my parents' love and approval. I did not want to feel rejected or criticized like my siblings. This also put a wedge between my siblings and me because my siblings resented me for acting so goody-good. What made matters worse is that I knew I was not this perfect child that my parents thought I was, but I could not let them see the real Cheryl inside because of my fear of their rejection.

By the time I was in my senior year of high school I had no peace because of so many internal conflicts. My English teacher decided that year that we were all to write our first term paper to get us ready for college and the topic she chose was "peace." Everyone in my class wrote on "world" peace but I heard a different drummer. I wanted to write on internal peace because I was desperate to find it. I recall going to the library to find a book on inner peace; however, I could not find one single book on the topic. I went to one of my teachers who loaned me one book she had, on which to base my paper. I basically wrote: "How can you have peace in the world if you don't have peace within your own soul."

During my high school years, I went to many priests and nuns seeking truth but very few could steer me in the right direction. I desperately wanted to know the truth. This search continued into my college years and long after as well.

During this time in my life, I loved going to church but I always felt that God was so far away on the other side of the stained-glass window. I knew He was worthy of my devotion, but I could not connect with Him. Except for that one encounter in the library, I felt a great distance and much silence between us. I felt like I was worshipping an austere far away God, not a loving personal one who wanted to be my friend and have an intimate relationship with me. I thought He was angry with me because of my saying no to Him that day in the library. I really felt like a fugitive running from God rather than a child running toward her Daddy God.

As my senior year was coming to an end, we all took the SAT to get into college. I really wanted to go to college to become a nurse. I loved hospitals and was a candy striper volunteer. My mom, however, who hated hospitals, told me that nursing was not a good career choice for me. After all, I could barely make it through high school math and science without a lot of help from teachers and students alike. She was right, but I really wanted to be a nurse. However, being a people-pleaser, I did what Mom told me I should do. She thought I would make a very good teacher. Despite my disagreement with her, I decided to go that route. I hit a stumbling block, however. I received very low scores on the SAT and without good scores no college would accept me; not even the local community college! Being at a loss, I went to a teacher whom I loved and asked for her advice. She told me to go to secretarial school instead but that was NOT what I wanted to do with my life. I hated typing class and did not do very well at it in school. Once again, I felt like a failure. My high school grades were good, and I graduated with a solid B average because I worked so hard. I took the leap and applied to a private Jesuit college; I was accepted however, "on probation".

A Step Back

Walking Down Memory Lane

As I look back on my life, as a child, I recall some treasured memories I would like to share with you. Even though I felt God was very far away, I still loved going to church. At Advent, we would always light the Advent candle wreath and say a prayer before our evening meal. Mom and Dad were very active in church functions and especially prayer meetings. Dad was a very active member of the Knights of Columbus and as little kids we always looked forward to that Sunday in Advent when we got to see Santa Claus at the Knights and receive our first Christmas gift.

Christmas also was a very special time for us. Dad worked very long hours during the weeks before Christmas at his store and we kids got to work there too. I loved my job of wrapping pretty gifts for people. Mom used to tell me I was a very creative wrapper and I made each gift look unique and beautiful. Dad also sold other

He Was There All the Time

things in his wholesale store at Christmastime, including toys. Being the oldest (when I got past the age of believing in Santa Claus) he allowed me to join him and Mom in picking out gifts for all my siblings. Then we would take them to a friend's house to be stored until that special day. Keeping a secret was such a challenge for me but it was worth the wait to see the excitement on my brother and sisters' faces when they opened their gifts from "Santa." In fact, one year I also was privy to another secret. Dad had invited a good friend of his to pose as Santa and come to our house Christmas eve. I had to go to bed early and pretend I was asleep so that my brother and sisters would fall asleep before he got there. The hour finally came around and Dad came running up the stairs to tell us excitedly that Santa had come early to pay our family a visit! What a sweet memory as we each got to sit on his lap and open a small Christmas gift. WOW!! A personal visit from Santa himself on such a busy evening!

Dad always made a big deal of decorating our home at Christmas time. We would go out and buy the biggest tree in town and then cut off a couple of feet from the top, so that it would fit perfectly in our family room. It was always a festive time for our whole family to decorate the tree and house so beautifully for our Savior's birth. It was truly a time of celebration which I always looked forward to with great anticipation. It took my mind off my dad and mom's problems and I would experience a natural high. It was also a sweet relief from the heavy pressure I felt inside my heart for my family, especially my dad. While decorating the house, Dad would play lovely Christmas music which we would sing along to while mom prepared our favorite traditional meal: Reubens and spicy eggnog. Mom was a great cook who always prepared a feast for our Christmas meal as well. We always invited others over -- especially those who had no family or place to go -- so our holidays were packed with laughter and lots of fun. But after the excitement of the holy day wore off, I felt that same depression surface in my heart once again.

Before we knew it, Valentine's Day rolled around, and Dad would always give each one of us a special Valentine candy which he chose from our favorite candy shop. You can't beat homemade fresh chocolates! We felt loved!

Soon enough Easter came, my next favorite Holy Day (but as I matured, it became my most favorite one). Easter was preceded by Lent and Dad's question to each of us: "What are you going to give up for Jesus and how are you going to draw closer to Him over these next forty days as we await His death and resurrection?" As crazy as it sounds, I LOVED Lent. It was not easy giving up our favorite dessert, but we always did this as a family. The best part of Lent was Holy Week. We would participate in various church services. On Holy Thursday, the priest would wash the feet of others in a special Last Supper service. I found this display of love so touching and beautiful that I wanted to do that for my husband on our wedding day if ever I was to be married. Good Friday was even more powerful for me. Dad would close his store from 12 noon to 3:00 PM so that we could attend a three-hour service commemorating the passion and death of Jesus. The priest would read the 7 last words of Christ and give a short homily after each word. It was a solemn but sobering time of reflection. I would think deeply about what Jesus did for me on that horrible day. I could not imagine how anyone could suffer the way He did out of pure love not only for me personally, but for all of us! It boggled my mind and heart. Then came the day we were all waiting for: Easter Sunday! He's alive and will never die again. Oh, what a happy day! The night before, mom and dad would fill our Easter baskets with all kinds of wonderful chocolates from our favorite chocolate shop and then hide them in hard to find places. What fun we had searching the house to find our basket only to be told we could not eat any of it until after Mass. I recall one year they hid one of the baskets in a bottom shelf in the kitchen. When my sister found her basket, it was almost empty with only wrappings left! What a tragedy to find out that our dog had a party the night before and she did not get sick and die!

Before Easter, Mom and Dad would take us out to buy an Easter outfit: new shoes and clothes to wear to Easter Sunday Mass.

After all, it was a time of new beginnings. Some years it felt wonderful to wear our new spring clothes on a warm Easter Day but how sad it was when often we had three feet of snow and had to return to our winter coats and boots! Yes, no matter the weather, it was truly a day of rejoicing and celebration and once again mom created a feast. The finest silverware and dishes came out, as well as the long awaited delicious desserts! But again, once all the excitement of Easter was over, the heavy sadness returned to my heart.

Another favorite time for me was the month of May. The flowers were finally blooming, and it was a special time of year for the church too. It is called Mary's month and we would have a beautiful May crowning of her statue, (at Sunday Mass), a symbol of her as Mother of God. I recall, as a very little girl, loving to make a little May altar for her by my bedside. I would look for the prettiest dandelions or other colorful flowers to place by her statue. I felt such a closeness to her and I did not really know why. I simply loved praying to her. To this day, these memories put a smile on my face. This also brings to mind- my First Holy Communion Day. I was blessed to pick out the most beautiful dress in all the world to receive Jesus into my heart, for the first time. I recall feeling like a little bride all decked up to meet my groom readying myself to give my heart totally to Him. Oh, what a very special day that was for me! I recall it being a warm, sunny

He Was There All the Time

day. My first Holy Communion Mass was followed by a big celebration at the Knights of Columbus. Yes, mom and dad made sure that this was a very special and memorable day in my life. Oh, how I wish my life could have stayed so pure and beautiful but, unfortunately, it did not. Believing the lies of Satan led me down some very wrong roads that led to much suffering and pain; however, what Satan meant for evil God has used for good in my life (See Romans 8:28). After much repenting, my life has gotten turned around and I have truly come to believe that God does write straight with crooked lines. Although I went off track as a young person, Jesus had a very special plan in all that has happened in my life. He wastes nothing and even uses our sins and sufferings for His purposes.

College & Beyond

I went to high school and college during the late 60's and early 70's, a time of great turbulence and confusion in the Catholic Church. Even though I went to a Catholic college, some of my teachers were quite liberal and did not follow orthodox, Catholic teachings. I was very naïve and impressionable, and easily influenced by them. During my freshman year, I had a teacher who did drugs for leisure but who was eventually dismissed from the school. One of the priests with whom I became friends was into Eastern religions and he invited me to his meetings. When my mom heard about this, she became very upset and told me I was being wrongfully influenced by this priest. Mom was very concerned that I was being pulled into eastern mysticism and I was! In searching for truth, I thought this would hold the answer for which I was searching. I was also involved in the Charismatic Renewal, which was starting up in the church during this time. Unfortunately, it did not satisfy the deep longing in my heart either!

He Was There All the Time

No matter who I talked to, that person had a different opinion about truth. I begged to know the "real truth" and, sad to say, I left college wondering if there was "a real truth" to be found. The 60's and 70's brought great confusion into my heart and mind.

I was required to take an Ethics class and the teacher taught us about situational ethics. He taught that there was no absolute right or wrong and that whatever felt right to us was right. We each had to do a project and bring in guests or talk about various issues revolving around different ethical issues. He gave us several suggestions and I chose homosexuality. Knowing nothing about this topic I decided to visit the local homosexuality community and invite two lesbian women to come speak to our class. It was a very difficult situation for me to accept yet we were being taught to keep an open mind. After all, there were no absolutes; everything was relative.

Unfortunately, by the time I graduated, I really wondered if God existed at all and I kept questioning which of these different approaches to life was right. I felt the way I was raised was old-fashioned religion and I needed to be part of the liberal open minded "do what you think and feel best" movement that many priests, nuns and other religious people were taking part of, in the church. After all, if the priests and nuns were doing these things how could it be wrong? I felt that I needed to keep up with the times. Sad to say, this feeling led me further away from the truth later in life because I was not anchored in my faith. I did not even know what the Catholic Church really believed because each teacher had his or her own opinion on what was right from real conservatism to extreme liberalism. I was like a boat being tossed to and fro on the sea of life and I just wished someone could throw me an anchor and steer my little boat in the right direction. How I wished someone could have told me what truth was. Unfortunately, I had to take the long, hard road and figure it out for myself. Mom tried to tell me, but I thought she was just being old-fashioned and very narrow minded!

My first semester in college was horrendous. I could not believe how hard college was. I was working part-time jobs, taking a full academic load and involved with extracurricular activities to help me "find myself." I recall joining ALSAC (Aiding Leukemia Stricken American Children), an organization that raised support for Danny Thomas's hospital for children. I linked up with a nun from our church and, at her suggestion, we decided to do a family fun fair to raise support for the hospital. As we got into the planning of it, she became very sick and had to back out; but she continued to guide me from her sick bed. I was overwhelmed with all the responsibility of putting together a fair in which I knew nothing about. Thank God, my dad helped me out, but the stress was still beyond my ability to cope. I remember one day thinking, "I can't handle life's stresses anymore." I was so depressed that one morning, as I was crossing the street in front of my college, I decided to run out in front of heavy traffic hoping I would get hit by a car. When I got to the other side unharmed, a school security guard who saw me pull this stunt came out of his booth yelling at me saying, "what are you trying to do? Get yourself killed?" Under my breath I said yes! I realized I needed help, so I went to a priest for guidance and, instead of helping me with my problems, he added to them by becoming a little too friendly with me. I could not believe this! I thought "who can I trust if not a priest?" I later found out that this priest left the priesthood to get married. I then sought out a school counselor who helped me cope with my crazy over whelming stress load. I got through the first semester and the fun fair went over very well, raising over $5,000.00 for the hospital. As good as I felt over this success, there was still a deep empty void in my heart.

Around November, of my freshman year I had another one of those "strange encounters" with the Lord. I went on a weekend Ignatian Retreat. It was a silent retreat held at our diocesan seminary in a very beautiful wooded, peaceful area. I went there searching for truth and inner peace. I wanted to be free of all this inner heaviness I had been carrying around in my heart and soul for so many years. We were only allowed to have our bible and a journal. The whole weekend was total silence. The spiritual director would give us a passage from the Bible for us to meditate on and then we would wait on the Lord to speak to our hearts. One very early morning, I walked out of the dorm to the cafeteria and, as I was walking across the campus, something very strange happened to me. Suddenly, I felt like I ran into a brick wall and my eyes were taken from me and I saw a vision. I had an out of body experience where I felt very light and free and beautiful. In the vision, I saw a very large group of people, all dancing in a circle holding upraised hands. The people were of all sizes, shapes, colors and nationalities. They were all ages too. They all seemed to be radiant and joyful. Then I heard a voice which said to me, "I am going to set you free and as I set you free, you are going to take someone else's hand and they are going to be set free and so on". Then there was a pause. Next thing I heard was "but it will be a long, slow process." With that my body returned into my body and I felt that great heaviness of heart and soul return as well. I recall saying as I looked off at the trees and hills that surrounded me, "But Lord why is it going to be a long, slow process?" He never answered that question. I can truly say that indeed it has been a very long, slow process.

I recall years later being told that getting set free is like peeling an onion one layer at a time. There are a lot of tears shed as we let go of the lies that we have come to believe and the deceptions with which we have fallen prey. There is a lot of dying to all the false things we believe about ourselves to get to the real person that God has created us to be.

College years had its ups and downs but academically it got better with each passing semester. By God's grace and much hard work, I graduated with a 3.65 average. This was the girl who was told she was not college material; BUT GOD had a different plan. As I trusted Him, He saw me through. In fact, in my junior year I was nominated for *Who's Who in America*, a very highly selective, prestigious honor society. I was being honored for all my extra-curricular activities, community service and good grades. My whole identity rested on these accomplishments and I wanted to make my parents so proud of me so that I could feel their love. Unfortunately, on the night of the election when the winners were announced, I was devastated that I was not one of the finalists. I felt my self-worth sink deep into a hole as I called my parents on the phone to tell them the very sad news. What made it worse was just before they announced the winners, I had called my parents to tell them how nervous I was, and they said do not be because we know you are going to be one of the finalists. Just believe it's a done deal. How shattered I was to call them back in tears to tell them this terrible news. Our hearts were broken that night, especially mine because I felt I had let them down! BUT GOD had another plan. A year later, I was nominated again, and I gave little credence to it after my previous let down. But to my amazement, I was selected. God works in His way and timing.

I want to share another strange encounter I had with God in my sophomore or Junior year – I cannot recall the exact timing of this event. I joined a teacher association and learned that some of my colleagues were taking drugs. Because of all the emotional pain I was going through, I thought about joining in; however, I did not, due to an "unusual encounter with God!" One early evening I was walking across the campus all alone; no one was around as I pondered the thought of whether I should join my friends in taking some drugs. Suddenly I heard a voice again which said: "Don't do it because it will hurt your future career." I remember arguing with the voice saying: "I'm only going to be a teacher like all these other people. What difference does it make?" Despite my lack of understanding, I decided not to do it and I am so glad I listened because it did affect a major career change later in my life.

Reflecting on some lighter moments, during my college years, I want to share a very funny story that happened to me. I was extremely shy, vulnerable and naïve. Having not been on many dates, I did not know how to act. A young man asked me on a date to see a movie at the local drive-in theatre. While I was focusing on the movie he was making advances toward me and I did not know what to do. I tried to push him away, but he kept pushing himself on me. Where was I to go, I thought? "Help me

He Was There All the Time

God, I don't know what to do!" Suddenly I heard a voice come from the big screen that sounded like my dad! I looked up and there was Dad on the screen! I couldn't believe my eyes. Was it a dream? Unbeknownst to me, my dad had placed an advertisement for his business with this theatre. I had to laugh that my dad came to my rescue just in the nick of time! I never saw that guy again!

During my junior year, I met a very nice young man who played the guitar and sang beautifully at our college's midnight Mass. I was so taken up with Marvin that I mustered the courage to talk to him. I found out he was a graduate of my college going into the army and waiting for orders. We started dating and he treated me so well. He was very kind and respectful and lots of fun to be with. After two years of dating, once I finished college, he asked me to marry him. I was so torn inside as I pondered this question because I felt our lives were going in very different directions. By then, he was in the army, while I felt a passionate burning in my heart to be a missionary. We talked about it and he suggested that I do "missionary work" in a soup kitchen or similar volunteer work like that, but my heart was telling me that I was being called to work as an overseas missionary. Of course, I had no plans and did not know if this would ever come to pass because I still did not want to be a nun and that was the only way to become a missionary! My heart was torn when I told him that I was not ready for marriage. We broke up amicably, but I felt deep pain in this separation and in our good bye. I thought to myself am I being a fool to chase after a pipe dream that might never come to pass? Perhaps my Dad was right. I AM heavenly bound and earthly worthless. Again, I sank into deep despair over this whole pipe dream of mine.

While dating, Marvin shared with me so often this wonderful little blessing from Numbers 6:22-26. It always brought me great peace and consolation especially after we broke up. In fact, whenever I read it in the Bible or heard it I always thought of Marvin. It says: "The Lord bless you and keep you! The Lord let His face shine upon you, and be gracious to you! The Lord look upon you kindly and give you peace!" Marvin and I agreed that whoever was to get married first would call the other.

I remember being enamored by Marvin's profession. Although he could not talk about it, I knew it had something to do with foreign intelligence. I used to secretly wish I could do something exciting like that rather than "just being an elementary teacher." But how did that thought fit in with being a missionary? Was I really a mixed up young woman or what? Perhaps God had a plan that I was not aware of at the time and this was just a small revelation of what was to come years down the road.

He Was There All the Time

My parents were involved in an international student exchange program during my teenage years and it was their desire to see my siblings and I go to a foreign country for a summer. I chose Peru. I did not speak Spanish very well so the family I was staying with suggested I go to language school to learn how to converse better with the people. I had lots of fun learning the language even though it was a difficult language to learn! One day while in the lady's restroom of the institute, I was chatting with my friend, who went with me on this exchange. Overhearing our conversation, a Spanish lady asked if we were from England. We proceeded to tell her we were from the United States. She said she knew someone from America; perhaps we might know as well. I thought to myself America is a huge country and what chances are we going to know this person! She told us he was a priest/missionary outside of Lima, Peru.

I almost fainted when she mentioned his name. Unable to hold the excitement in, I proceeded to tell her I had written to him years ago when I was in high school and had lost touch with him. I had totally forgotten that he was working as a missionary in Peru. I then asked her if she could get me in touch with him. She said he worked far away in the countryside whereas we were in Lima, the capital. But she would try and sure enough she made the connection between us. This wonderful priest met me and took me all around his area, introducing me to his very poor people. I was blessed to see their very humble homes and beautiful, simple church. I just loved it. The people were so very friendly and gracious to me. I felt like I was in a dream. Only God could have put this divine connection together and once again I felt sure that this was what I wanted to do with my life. However, how would this happen if I did not want to be a nun for the rest of my life. Oh, poor me! I was a pitiful mess. I wanted so badly to go back and visit him again, but he was very busy and lived far away from where I was staying. BUT GOD once again worked another one of his mysterious miracles.

One day, while going home from school on the public city bus someone pick pocketed me and stole my instamatic camera with all my wonderful pictures of this priest and our day together. I cried and was so upset because that had been the highlight of my experience in Peru! Seeing how upset I was, my "mother" (the lady I was staying with) said we'll try to get you another camera and see if you can go visit him again. Sure enough, she pulled some strings and we were once again together for another day. To further solidify my desires to return to Peru as a missionary, my mother was a widow who loved spending her time helping the poor. These people lived in caves and had practically nothing, yet they were so happy and full of the love of God. They were very humble holy people and they ministered to me, just like the wonderful people with whom my priest friend worked. I was convinced this was truly my life-calling. I wanted to be like my "Mom" and do what she and this priest were doing. Only time would tell what God (not Cheryl) had in mind.

I recall leaving college disillusioned, confused, empty and very distrusting of people because everyone decided what truth was for themselves. I felt my Catholic education left me life-less inside; however, this experience put me on a journey to find truth and inner peace for myself. I started taking yoga lessons which left me peaceful and relaxed yet still empty inside. I delved into Eastern meditation and mysticism and even went on a retreat given by nuns who combined Eastern mysticism and Catholic spirituality. But something inside me told me this was not the answer either! I really enjoyed the experiences but the little red caution light in my heart told me to steer clear of this type of thing. I felt sad about it because I was really getting into it. For a while, I was even meditating on candles but still no peace!

For a period of time, I went church hopping from extreme liberal churches to very strict orthodox churches. How could there be such vast differences between these Catholic churches. Depending the pastor, I received mixed messages, especially when it came to moral issues. Through some friends, I started to drift toward the Protestant faith. My mom was very upset with me telling me this was a serious mistake on my part; however, I loved their prayer meetings and worship! The people were so joyful and alive, and I felt like my heart and spirit were being ministered to. I struggled with my mom's warning to me. I feared leaving the Catholic Church, but I felt I was being fed and I was coming alive in ways I had not experienced before. I was desperate to breathe life and get away from all the turbulence going on in the various Catholic churches. Some of my friends were even into cults and I decided to check these out too. I kept telling myself these friends of mine are very highly educated successful people and if they think it's OK, it must be OK. By this time, my Mom was very concerned with my drifting and she bought me a book on cults which I read. That book opened my eyes to what cults were all about, so I quit searching in those directions despite my friends' attempts to join their churches.

I wondered how could all these fine people be deceived? I found my solace in the Protestant churches. I continued to go to their prayer meetings on occasion and to the Catholic Church on Sundays. Fear of going to hell gripped my heart, not love of God and wanting to be at Mass to worship Him. Over the years, I found myself drifting more toward the Protestant faith. I didn't decide one day to just leave my Catholic faith. A series of life experiences just led me in that direction. The struggle still raged in my heart because I was learning to hear the voice of the Lord and learning how to walk in His ways. Yet it was happening in a way I never expected. Jesus was truly becoming my personal, intimate friend whom I could trust. The struggle came when a small voice inside me would say this is not pure truth. Only the Catholic Church holds the whole truth. But why was I not getting it when I attended the Mass or other services. Over time, I did drift just to stay emotionally and spiritually alive despite this inner conflict. I recall being told by someone that the Catholic Church was like whole wheat brown bread and the Protestant churches were like white bread. Both were nourishing and good, but the brown bread was better for me. But why was the white bread feeding my soul so much more than the wholesome brown bread?

Teaching Years

Despite good grades, honors and great recommendations, I was unable to secure a teaching job after college. Elementary school teaching jobs were very difficult to find. There were too many teachers and very few openings. I had submitted over 80 applications and nothing materialized. In desperation, I substitute taught for several months. I found this one school I absolutely loved but again, no openings. Then one day, God did for me what I could not do for myself. I was attending a prayer meeting at my church and I met a lady who happened to attend our prayer meeting "just this one time." As we were talking, she told me about her aunt who was a principal of a Catholic school. She wanted to put me in touch with her to see if she had any openings in her school. Sure enough, she had a first-grade opening and immediately I clicked with this wonderful elderly nun who hired me for $3,000.00 a year. WOW! My first real job. I could teach very well but discipline was another story. She came to my rescue on more than one occasion. Given another situation, I might have been fired! She came to love me, and was on my side to see me succeed when I wanted to give up on teaching all together. With her encouragement, I stuck it out and moved with my students to 2nd grade the following year. That year was much better, and I ended up loving it.

I must share a very funny story about this sweet nun. We became very good friends and occasionally we would go out to dinner. One night, as we were driving to the restaurant, we saw a man stopped on the side of the thruway. Using our less than better judgment, we decided to stop and help him. When we pulled up, he seemed taken aback seeing this nun in a habit and if he had any evil intentions they were subdued when he saw her. It turned out he had car troubles and needed to get to a gas station. No cell phones back in the 70's! All went well but I learned you just don't help strangers even if you are a nun in a black habit! Unless of course the Lord tells you to do so, then you just obey and trust Him.

Another funny story-- I was very low on cash, but I wanted to take Sister out to a nice restaurant for dinner. I decided I would have enough money if I ordered the cheapest thing on the menu. To my surprise, she suggested that we order an appetizer and our meals too! I was choked up the whole dinner wondering how I was going to pay for all this food that I was not expecting. Despite my anxiety, I had just enough to pay the bill. Next time, I would borrow from Dad before taking Sister out to a nice restaurant. After all, how often did she really get to go out to nice restaurants for dinner? You live and learn to expect the unexpected!

Sister and I had many deep talks during our times together and I began sharing my dreams of becoming a missionary. I told her of my struggles about becoming a nun and I really wondered if I should just do it! She flat out told me not to become a nun! She never went into much detail; she just said that she thought it was not a good choice for me. I thought this was a bit strange coming from a very godly woman, but I tucked that advice in the back of my mind. Also, while teaching at this school, I became very good friends with another teacher who was a former nun herself and she told me that being a nun was not at all what I thought. Life in the convent was very hard and she almost had a breakdown and eventually left the convent. She told me her sister also was a nun and she too ran into difficulties and left the convent and went on to become a principal of a public school. If I was confused before, now I was really confused about religious life. I thought nuns were almost as holy as Jesus, yet these three ladies saw it quite differently!

As much as I loved the school where I was teaching, I knew I had to find a better paying job, so I applied to my church school which paid me a little more than I was making. Unfortunately, I was offered a job teaching science, (my worst subject) to 5th graders.

He Was There All the Time

I told the principal that I was not good in science, but he told me that was the only opening he had. He gave me a night to pray and think about it. I went into serious prayer and asked the Lord what to do. He gave me total peace and I felt He was going to teach me science so that I in turn could teach it to these kids. Well this turned out to be my best teaching year because I had no idea what I was doing, yet God kept giving me these great ideas and the kids loved them and so did I. The next year an opening occurred in Kindergarten, which was my dream job. But when I got it, I was totally disillusioned and disappointed. It was not as fulfilling as teaching science to my fifth graders. I taught these little ones in my own strength and experience whereas I taught science in total dependence on the Lord and His strength.

Despite the fact, that I was burned out of studying, I had to go back to school to get my Master's Degree if I wanted to continue teaching in New York State. Therefore, I took the GRE (Graduate Record Exam) only to face my worst fears once again: very poor scores. I wanted to teach Special Education (Special Ed) and the school I applied to accepted me, but said I could not join that department because I had no prior teaching credentials in that area. They suggested I go into the reading specialist program. I went to that dean and, when she saw my low GRE scores, said I would never make it through the program. I assured her I could do it based my college grades, but she insisted I just get my

Masters in Elementary Education and forget the reading specialist program. She set me up in the regular education program much to my dismay. I remember leaving her office crying: "Why, Lord, why?" When I got to my car I finally said: "OK Lord I surrender to Your will. If this is what You want for me, I accept it. Thy will be done." I felt sad but free. I let my dream go.

I was soon busily into my program and enjoying it. Then I hit another roadblock. One day, I went into a class that the dean had put on my schedule and the professor said the class was for reading specialists only and all others were asked to leave. I told him I was following the curriculum that the dean placed me on, so I didn't know why the mix-up. He then said, "What is your name? Let me check my roster to see if you are on it." To my shocking surprise, my name was on it! The dean must have had a change of heart after my talk with her but never informed me that she changed my program to what I really wanted! After two years, not only did I get my Master's Degree as a reading specialist, but I graduated with a 4.0 average! Once again, I recalled what the dean told me: that if I took this program I would not succeed at it. BUT GOD had another plan. Little did I know how this program was going to help me later in my life.

This period in my life proved to be very difficult indeed. Not only was I teaching full time, going to classes at night, and writing my Master's thesis but I was still trying to figure out my future. I really wanted to resolve these issues that had burdened me for so many years: being a nun to fulfill my dream of being a missionary or being happily married and raising a large family of our own, including special needs children. I still struggled over my sexual issues as well: being celibate or living a sexually fulfilling life as a married woman. What was God's will for me anyways?

Once again, I sought out what I thought was a wonderful priest. I had heard him give a talk and he seemed approachable and easy to talk to. After the meeting was over, I asked him if we could talk sometime. He gladly responded with a "yes of course -- just give me a call and set up an appointment." I did just that and we met. I told him that I wanted to be a missionary, but I felt no desire to be a nun because of the struggles I had with my sexuality issues, and that I dreamed of being happily married with lots of kids and adopting special needs kids as well. Then he went on to say that he could help me with these issues. He began by saying that the bible says, "Love and do as thou wilt." I didn't quite understand what he meant by that until he went on. He said, "I want to help you with your sexual issues so that you can make a good decision about your future." I naively trusted him. However, I did not experience healing at all. Rather, I felt ashamed for allowing myself to fall into one of Satan's lies. It has taken me years to forgive myself and him but, through the grace of God, I have been able to let God bring deep inner healing to my wounded soul.

Years later, I found out that he had died, so I pray for his soul often.

I blamed myself and felt it was my entire fault that this happened. After all, I was in my early 20's and not a child! Because of this self-condemnation, I found it very difficult to forgive myself. How could God ever forgive me? That relationship not only damaged me emotionally, but it also opened the door to further problems later in my life. I felt like I went from being a trusting, naïve, goody-good girl to a horrible sinner. Needless to say, I stuffed all of this pain deep within the recesses of my heart, not telling a soul about it for many years. I felt God would never bless me and I wondered what kind of a future awaited me. Would God punish me forever or would He be the God of second chances? Because I felt so dirty inside, I did not feel God could love me causing self-rejection to emerge in my heart.

One summer night while studying for one of my exams the phone rang, and I did not want to interrupt my studies, but I answered the phone anyway only to get the call I dreaded! It was Marvin calling to tell me he kept our promise to call the other if one of us was getting married first. I was so happy for him and I knew the woman he was marrying would be tremendously blessed, but I was very sad for me because I had let him go to follow my crazy pipe dream. I really began to think perhaps I was "heavenly bound and earthly worthless". After all, where had my life gone in the two years since we had broken up. I wished him well and just cried and cried after we hung up.

During this time, one of my younger sisters was looking for a job in criminal justice, so I went with her to an interview with the FBI. I sat outside the door while she went in for her lengthy interview. When she came out she said: "Forget it. I don't want the secretarial job because they want to send me to Washington, DC" and she wanted to stay home because of a relationship she was in. I thought to myself, I wish I could do that, but I did not major in criminal justice. Now why would I have thought such a ridiculous thing when I really wanted to be a missionary? I just thought she was giving up a great opportunity for a guy (whom she eventually married)!

Sometime after that, I was attending a woman's prayer meeting with my mom and a lady came up to mom and asked about my sister. She said: "I know your daughter majored in criminal justice; has she ever thought of joining the FBI? They are now looking for women to serve as special agents." Her daughter was now an agent and just loved it! Mom told her that my sister had checked into it but did not want to leave the area. I asked her what her daughter majored in to get into the FBI. I was floored when she said she was a teacher. A teacher? You mean they are taking other people besides attorneys, accountants and people with criminal justice backgrounds? And she said YES! I asked her how to apply. I wanted to try out myself! Not only did I shock my Mom, but I shocked myself as well. Why would I be doing this? It made no logical sense, but I felt it was right. I applied and went down to the same office I had taken my sister. I was told I had to take two exams: one a very difficult English exam and the other a psychological exam to see if I was "agent material". I was not at all surprised when the results came back: "We are sorry we cannot consider you because you did not do very well on the English exam; however, you did extremely well on the psychological exam. Without being a good writer, you just can't be a good agent." But in my heart, I knew that I was a very good writer; this exam once again did not reveal my true ability. Although saddened by this news, I just chalked it up as a closed door that was not meant to be.

I was teaching kindergarten when this whole FBI situation took place. By the end of my school year, I had another shocker. Dad, a very strong controlling type of person, said to me: "Cheryl you are too comfortable in this school and you need to quit and move on." I was frightened to leave my very cozy job in this wonderful school, but he was right. He told me that if I did not resign, I probably would never leave. After all, I now had a master's degree in reading and I needed to find a job in that field. After applying to many schools, nothing happened. Then out of the blue, I received a call from my favorite school system and I was so excited. It was the one I had subbed for a few years prior. In fact, not only was I being interviewed by this school system, but they wanted to hire me for my very favorite school in that school system! I couldn't believe it. This was truly a God incident because no other school system called me for an interview!

When it was time for the principal to interview me, I was told that he was on vacation and another principal would do the interview. That day I was wearing a Holy Spirit pin on my lapel and the principal happened to notice it. She asked if I was a Christian and I told her I was. She then went on to tell me she was too! I could not believe it. The interview went from being formal to very informal in a matter of minutes. There was an instant connection between us and we started sharing our faith journeys. She told me the superintendent had to interview me and he would make the final decision. She further told me that I would be teaching at the other school, but I would teach two afternoons at her school and that is why she interviewed me. I was very nervous about my interview with the superintendent but as I was waiting for him to call me into his office, I was reading a book called *"Abandonment to Divine Providence".* How timely that I should come to a page that talked about letting go and abandoning my life to the Lord, so I decided then and there to do just that! I let go and left the whole situation to God. I thought, once again, if it is meant to be then the Lord would open the door and if not then I knew it was not His will. With that mindset, I went into the interview and shortly thereafter I was hired without even meeting the primary principal with whom I was going to work! This whole experience was truly a God incident and my whole year there proved to be so. I made some wonderful friends and I loved the poor students I was teaching. I knew how they felt because I too struggled with reading myself while in school. They could feel my love and compassion for them and I saw why God led me into this field and not nursing. He is so good and wise. Despite my frustration with my Mom, in telling me that I would make a better teacher than nurse, I had to admit she was right! Out of my own struggles, I was better able to help others with similar difficulties. Little did I know what the Lord was preparing me for years down the road.

Things were going very well for me until one late January morning. The phone rang about 7:00 AM as I was getting ready for school and I wondered who would be calling this early. I answered it only to hear some man say he was a Special Agent with the FBI and that he was looking for me. I thought this was a joke that one of my friends was playing on me because they knew I had applied the year before but didn't get in. I thought, however, why would they be playing a trick on me so early in the morning? I questioned him as to the purpose of his call and he said that I was being offered a job with an upcoming new agent class in March. "What?" I said. When I realized he was telling the truth, I asked how could

He Was There All the Time

this be since I was turned down a year earlier. He went on to explain a policy change that had occurred in the FBI since I first applied. The FBI had determined someone could be taught to be a good writer, but that person could not necessarily be taught how to be a good agent. Either a person has what it takes, or they do not, and he said because I did very well on the psychological exam, I was just the kind of person the FBI was looking for. Then came the test! He said that the Bureau wanted me to begin training in March. I could not believe that my life was being turned upside down by one phone call! As I pondered his offer, I said to him, I cannot take it because I want to finish off my school year contract. This was a serious decision because I had a good job in my field, and in order for me to be permanently certified as a reading teacher, I had to get two years of teaching experience in the field of remedial reading. Even if I took the job, I would be losing the second year that I needed to complete my permanent certification. As I shared with him my concern, he said that he would call FBI Headquarters in Washington, DC to see if they would give me an extension to finish off my school year. He told me that he would have an answer by the next morning. The call came as expected and he said they affirmed that decision. I would finish teaching on a Friday in June and immediately head to the FBI Academy at Quantico, Virginia, that weekend to start classes on the following Monday! Then came the background check. I now realized what that still small voice was talking about back in college when I heard the Lord say: "Don't take the drugs because it will affect your future job!" Little did I ever dream I would be going into the FBI as a Special Agent. Me? Quiet church mouse me who is so "much afraid?" How can this be? I never even fired a gun in my life nor was I a physical fitness buff! In fact, I hated physical exercises and sports in school and used to take the easiest gym classes with which I could get away! Now I was going to be stretched to my limit and beyond!

BUT GOD once again came to my rescue with His amazing plan. My cousin knew of a guy who ran a gym for body builders -- I mean real body builders who competed in boxing tournaments. "Much afraid" (the name I endearingly call myself) went down to the gym only to discover that another young man had gone there before me to prepare for the FBI as well. The coach knew exactly what I needed to do to get prepared for Quantico. I could not help but believe that this was a divine connection. All I kept thinking is that this must be God's will for me because everything was falling into place so smoothly. Although none of this made sense with my life dreams, it all felt so right -- until I got started. I could barely run a lap, yet I had to run two miles in less than 16 minutes at Quantico. I also had to learn to do push-ups, pull ups, sprints and many other challenging things in a certain amount of time. But my coach knew exactly what to do to get me ready for June. He was not going to let me give up when I wanted to. He would keep pushing me past the impossible and I thank God, he did!

During this time, I also signed up for judo, karate and boxing classes at another gym to help prepare me for those daunting tasks that lie ahead. Those were five very stressful months that I thought would never come to an end. Finally, June rolled around and one of my friends told me her husband was a hunter and that he would teach me how to use a handgun before I started my FBI training. That helped get me over the shakiness of holding a real gun. Would I ever have to use this thing I thought? I hoped never; but still I had to know how to be ready in case the time should come that I would have to shoot someone. Oh God, forbid! What was I thinking or doing with my life?? This was very serious business. As crazy as it sounds I still had peace inside that this was where I was meant to be. Little did I know at the time how this was preparing me for something else God had in mind for me later in life.

The day came when I had to face my sweet principal who hired me just one year earlier and tell her I was leaving my wonderful job. I was scared to face her because of the great relationship we had. She knew I loved my job so why would I be leaving? But I had to be honest and tell her that I was not looking for this job with the FBI. It just came to me in a most bizarre way! I explained the whole story and she just nodded her head saying I was about to throw away my whole Master's Degree by not staying and getting my second year of experience. Without that second year of experience, I would never be permanently certified, so I knew the risk was great. Out of concern, she asked if I was aware of the gravity of my decision. I told her that I had prayerfully thought through this whole decision and I knew it was right. I just needed to do it. I left her office very downcast, but I knew I had to go forward and "do it afraid."

During my few months of preparation for the FBI, I did take seriously this life change. In fact, I even went on my own contemplative retreat. I went to a retreat center in the country and stayed in a little prayer cabin by myself, praying and fasting on bread, water and tea for several days seeking the Lord's will. I brought my Bible, journal and some other spiritual reading material. I asked the Lord for confirmation that I was truly hearing from Him and this was His will for me. It was a life change bigger than anything I had ever done before. I did not want to make a mistake. I was dating a guy who I was serious about before the FBI came into my life. Therefore, I had some serious praying to do about that too! The Lord answered my prayer in a very strange way during the retreat. Unbeknownst to me, I had picked up a meditation booklet and when I opened it up, it was talking about the FBI and its founder. I learned about its work and what a great organization it was. Of all the things to bring with me, I never dreamed I would be reading something about the FBI in one of my meditation books! Again, I saw this as a God incident that I could not ignore. By the end of the retreat, my mind was made up and I was sure I was doing the right thing. I told my boyfriend I had to go forward with this plan and, although we were both sad, he accepted my decision. In fact, before we dated, he had been in the seminary and had left but after we broke up he joined another order and went on to become a fine priest. Years later, I had the privilege of attending his ordination.

I Did It Afraid

FBI Days

Over the years, I have been asked what ever led me into this kind of work. As I think back on it, I really believed it would help me become more assertive, confident and independent. I was not the macho, aggressive type that you think of when you think of FBI agents! I was the very opposite: reserved, quiet and a very deep, intuitive thinker. When I would tell people that I was going into the FBI, most people who knew me were shocked and said, "it's just not you!" However, I knew something deep inside was saying it was me and that it was preparing me for even bigger things ahead. In a very strange sort of way, I felt like this was a stepping stone but to what I did not know. At the time, I had no idea what that something might be! I thought perhaps it would help prepare me to be a missionary. I would travel, and experience adventure every day because no two days would ever be alike. I get bored easily with routines and I love continual change, so this felt like the perfect job. I also thought that I would be able to pay off my school loans more quickly, so I could be debt free when I felt ready to move forward toward my ultimate dream.

Monday came too fast. Goodbyes to my family were very hard because I felt so close to them and --except for my two months in Peru -- I had never been away from them for very long. I was not the independent type at all. I had no idea how to stand on my own two feet. But now I had to grow up real fast and act like a big girl and a big girl I was not! In fact, I was the smallest woman in my class in both size and stature. I was also the most fragile and delicate. To help prepare me for Quantico, dad gave me one of his large belts to hold my holster because he knew mine were too thin. When I arrived there, we all had to be fitted for grays or fatigues, but they ran out of women's clothing, so they gave me a men's small which proved to be way too big! A seamstress took the pants in and the back pockets almost touched. As a result, I came to be known as "hip pockets," to my firearms instructor.

Then came the big test. We had to run an obstacle course and jump over a high wall -- but I was too short to climb it -- and all in a very short period of time! I was not prepared for this, so I had no idea how to even do it. When our physical education (PE) instructor -- who was a seven-degree black belt -- saw that I was too short, he allowed one of the men to cup his hands so that I could at least jump from his hands over the wall. It was all timed and I barely did it huffing and puffing. Then came the two-mile run. My classmates were all so fast compared to me. How foolish I was to think I was well prepared. My PE instructor was also our karate, judo and boxing instructor and he came down real hard on me probably because I was so fragile and petite. He knew the kind of criminals I would be coming up against and he knew he had to prepare me for this kind of "combat!" He loved embarrassing me in front of my classmates to try to motivate me to do better. He was never encouraging but kept telling me I was not good enough. He would tell me that I would never make it in the real world if I did not make it in his class. He was right, in retrospect, but I could not handle his continual negative approach to learning. I was very sensitive and took his remarks personally. Oftentimes I would just leave the class crying and wondering what I was doing there. As a teacher, my approach was so very different when it came to motivating people to do their best or to try harder. For one thing, I never humiliated struggling students in front of their peers and I never compared the slower students to the smarter ones. My job was always to come along side and encourage the weaker ones to try harder and do their best with my encouragement and help. This was a rude awakening for me!

As challenging as PE training was, firearms training was just as difficult, if not worse in some respects. The first day on the firing range, one of the agents who was spotting me from behind, came up and started distracting me by focusing on my belt. He mocked me, saying I was probably wearing my dad's belt (little did he know he was right). I was so humiliated, I just wanted to run off the field, but I sucked up my tears and kept shooting. Then he said sarcastically: "You're shooting at the birds in the air and not the target." On the other hand, my firearms instructor was like a father to me in that he was very encouraging and patient with my inability to always hit the target. He gave me a pistol that did not shoot bullets and he told me how to hold it and to imagine I was shooting at a target. I would go back to my dorm room and practice. When mid-term qualifications came, I barely passed but I was motivated to work all the harder so that I would pass the final qualification test.

In the meantime, my PE instructor continued to humiliate me in front of my peers by having me run in front of the whole class so everyone else was practically walking at a snail's pace. Then my classmates would all start yelling at me to run faster but this did not help me to speed up; it just made the class angrier at me for slowing everyone else down. During judo class, he would deliberately put me with the biggest guy in the class and tell me I had to flip him over my body. It was outrageous, and my partner would say I will flip myself over you.

Often I would run alone during my own practice time and one day this thought came to me: "I have had enough of this life. I am going to quit. I just cannot take all this harassment anymore. My principal was right. This is not the life for me. I will go back home and be a teacher again." Immediately, I heard a still small voice out of the blue say: "I never said that it would be easy, but I promise to see you through." That little message has helped me so much throughout my life when I have found myself in difficult or impossible situations.

The academic classes at Quantico also were very hard. I had never studied law and now I had to learn all these federal laws, along with such subjects as the psychology of the criminal mind. My own mind was on stress overload. Thank God for the *Globe and Laurel* down Richmond Highway from the Academy. On weekends, my classmates would go there just to get away from the stress. I was not a drinker, per se, but I would join in for a glass of wine and then go for my soda. But my classmates would buy me more drinks to help me relax and I kept saying no, no. But one night, I gave in and drank more than my usual and boy was I very sick. Never again did I allow them to keep pushing me beyond my limit.

I did have a couple of wonderful experiences with some of my classmates, however. One day, one of the fastest women in my class offered to run with me. She made running look so easy and I could not believe that I was actually able to keep up with her! Why could I do this with her yet alone, I could not run very fast at all? It just shows the power of support and encouragement.

He Was There All the Time

Another time, one of the men offered to run with me from behind and he just lightly tapped my back with his finger tips and I felt like I was floating on air. My feet felt so light. But again, left to myself, I went back to my snail's pace. It just showed me how I needed others if I was going to make it through Quantico. Whenever we were running on the track, we had to pass a sign on a tree that read "no pain, no gain." How true that was for me, for sure!

Despite the still small voice speaking words of encouragement to me, about half way through the program, I went to our class counselor and told him I was quitting and going home. He was shocked to hear this and said I was doing fine. I couldn't believe we were talking about the same person. He asked me why I was quitting. I told him that I was barely passing firearms and that the PE program was way too challenging for me and I just could not keep up with my classmates. My academic classes were very hard also, but I was pulling a solid "B" average. He encouraged me to take the weekend off, fly home, think about it and let him know Monday morning. While at home, my dad had a very stern talk with me. He said: "Sherry, if you quit at this what else are you going to quit at when life gets tough? Also, if you quit what are you going to come back to, knowing how hard it was to find teaching jobs in our area? Plus, if you quit you will never know what you could have had, had you stuck it out. Now go back and finish the course that you started." The next day, my dad put me on a plane and sent me back to Quantico. As hard as this was, I am so glad that my Dad talked sternly with me. I needed to seriously think about this life decision and the impact it would have on my future.

Somehow, when final qualification day came, by God's grace, I did pass all the PE as well as the firearms requirements. God blessed me in the academic area as well. I passed all my final exams.

Upon graduation, I reported to my first assignment and was quickly met by real agents and the real world of criminals. I was assigned to the criminal squad with these macho cop type agents. I worked on many bank robbery cases but there are two that stand out in my mind.

I was a brand-new agent, a rookie, just out of training school and I was excited to go on a real arrest of an alleged bank robber. We arrived at the man's house about 6:00 AM and the agents were going to knock on his front door and hope he would open it without incident and then they would arrest him. There were three big guys and me. When we got to the house the lead agent told me that I was to stand guard at the back door while the other three would guard the front door. He said that if the man did not answer the door they were going to break down his door. I followed orders and stood post waiting to hear what to do next. While standing there I thought: what if the bank robber runs out of the back door?

He Was There All the Time

I prayed for protection and I asked the Lord to please watch over me and help me because I did not know if I would be strong enough to drag this man down and arrest him all alone. I had learned in class that you only use the gun when your life is in danger. I was going to have to use all those judo and karate skills my PE teacher pounded into me. Now I knew why he came on so hard with me. I had to be prepared for such a situation as this, but I did not feel at all ready! I leaned on my Lord, instead. I prayed that He would fight for me and He did! Upon finishing my prayer, one of the agents came back and said nothing was happening so he was relieving me to go up front. No sooner had I gotten to the front door, we heard a ruckus in the back yard. The alleged bank robber had just run out the back door right into his own arrest with a big, strong seasoned agent that was able to hold him down and arrest him. WOW I learned the power of prayer again and God's protection that day!

Another time I was given my own bank robbery case. An elderly man tried robbing a bank but to his surprise the local police department was right next door to the bank and the police immediately arrested him and turned him over to us as bank robbery is a federal crime. My supervisor assigned the case to me and told me to arrest him and place him in jail. Fresh out of Quantico, I had my first real opportunity to handcuff someone and nervously I tried to do it right. I did not want him to think I was a rookie and that he was my first arrest! Being so nervous I put the handcuffs on too tight. The next day his wife came to me quite upset because the handcuffs almost cut off his circulation and left marks on his wrists. I felt badly about this especially when she told me he was a good man who never even had a driving ticket. I wondered why he tried robbing a bank. I came to find out that he owned a business that was having financial problems and he started to have emotional problems over his situation. Fortunately, he was given a pre-trial diversion. Instead of going to jail he was going to do some community service and get counseling to help him with his problems. I was so happy with this outcome and I'm sure his wife was too. I hope she eventually forgave me!

One day, I came back to the office from following up on one of my leads and there was a message on my desk taken by one of the other agents. He said that I had gotten a call on my phone while I was out, so he took the message for me. It was from Mr. Lion. I thought I don't know a Mr. Lion and I wasn't waiting for any information from a man by that name. But I returned the call anyway. The whole squad broke out into roaring laugher when the person on the other side of the phone said: "City Zoo!" I should have known these guys were up to something. They used to say that I belonged in the convent and not the FBI! I was just so gullible and naïve, and they knew it! Over time, we all became good friends and had lots of laughs together.

He Was There All the Time

But I knew this kind of work was not for me. I was not the "macho type" at all. I really wanted to work on another squad where they did foreign counter-intelligence work rather than police work. Over time, I proved myself and the agent in charge transferred me and I found my niche in the counter-intelligence department. I loved it! Thinking back, I realized this was another God incident. Only God could have opened this door for me. I thought back to when I dated Marvin and I remembered wishing I could do similar work as him (although I never really knew what that work was). It just sounded so exciting and I never dreamed in a million years I would be doing a similar kind of work years later. What's even more amazing is that God was training me in this field for something much bigger years down the road!

One day I got a call from an old friend from college days who found out I was now working for the FBI. He asked if I could join him and his wife for dinner and I was overjoyed to reconnect until I found out why! He told me that, while in college, he was working with an FBI agent providing him with "classified information." I thought this was a big joke until I went back to the office and discovered that we, in fact, had a file on him and that he had worked with one of my partner agents! He begged me for information about his file but due to security reasons, I was unable to tell him anything. I never heard from him again! After this funny incident, I just shook my head thinking that one of my college friends was an undercover spy for the FBI! Who would have thought...and now I was working for the FBI as well but in a very different capacity!

Transfer time came, and I was assigned to another field office and to my amazement I was placed in the counter-intelligence department again. I was so happy about this new assignment. Having never lived on my own, I asked my dad to go with me on my very first house hunting trip. Not only did I have to look for an apartment, but I also had to look for furniture to fill my new home. Dad was an expert in this field because he was in the wholesale business and knew all about furniture. I was so excited when we found the apartment of my dreams in a wooded area but close enough to work. It was brand new and I got first pick. Now for the furniture I wanted. Dad said that he and mom wanted to bless me by buying the furniture so all I had to do was pick it out and have it delivered after I moved there. We went to the lower end of the city to the furniture district and I found my perfect set of furniture for every room. I was elated until we went to check out. When we went to pay, the salesman noticed that my Dad was wearing a Christian pin on his coat (sound familiar?) He asked if he was a Christian and Dad said very proudly, yes! The salesman then whispered -- so that no one could hear him -- that he could not sell us the furniture. Shocked and saddened we asked why? He said that his friend owned the store and it was a front for drugs and we would never see the furniture, so he was warning us before we got

He Was There All the Time

badly burned. He told us that he worked for his friend hoping he would convert him to the faith! What a way to come into a new city! If this guy only knew that I was in the business of running down drug dealers! Again, another God incident! He further directed us to other furniture stores up the street and we finally found one run by two elderly people. My dad felt very comfortable working with these folks and together we furnished my new home with furniture far more beautiful than the first place. How wonderful things work out when we trust the Lord with our desires and needs. He gives us more than we can dream or hope for.

I moved to my new assignment and city in January in the middle of a treacherous snow storm. No sooner had I gotten out there and my car went dead and the movers could not deliver my furniture. I was living out of a few boxes of things I had brought with me! This was not a fun way to move into a new city and to have no support from family or friends. I felt so alone and scared. I did what I had done so many times before -- I cried out to God in prayer. To my surprise, He answered my prayer in a way I never expected. My boss came to me within the first few weeks of being on the job and said he was assigning me to a temporary undercover drug case in another state, where the weather was much warmer! I was delighted to leave the snow behind for the next few months. Moreover, having never worked drugs, I also was excited about the change in assignments.

When I arrived at the local field office, I was told that I would need a rental car during my stay so one of the agents took me to a rental office in another part of the city. I was following the lead agent back to the office on the very busy highway when traffic cut me off and I ended up going onto another highway and, with no GPS in those days, I had to trust signs and intuition. Unfortunately, I ended up in a very poor section of town and I sensed it was not a good place to be. I stopped at a rundown gas station and asked the attendant if he knew where the FBI office was. He nodded and started speaking to me in Spanish! Although I had spent two months in Peru years ago, I did not understand what this man was saying. I got back into my car and once again, prayed in desperation to God to lead me back to the office. I don't know how it happened, but He got me there with my head hanging low as I walked into the office about an hour late for our meeting and assignments. Fortunately, nothing was said to me and I felt relieved!

It was Sunday, February 14th and I was settling into my hotel room exhausted over the events of the past couple of days. I called a friend to tell her of my tale of woes since my transfer and how I missed my family and friends. I was feeling very lonely and depressed. A couple of hours into our conversation, I realized I had missed dinner and was hungry, so she recommended that I get some food. It was about 9:00 PM and I felt like a McDonald's

He Was There All the Time

burger, so I headed out to a nearby restaurant I had seen earlier in the day. When I returned to the hotel, I pulled into a parking spot and again heard that voice with which I had become so familiar. The voice said: "Do not get out of the car!" Another car had pulled into the hotel after me, but I thought they too were looking for a spot also. I was wrong!! I ignored that still small voice arguing with myself as to why I should not get out of the car. No sooner had I opened my door, a man jumped out of his car and grabbed for my purse. Immediately the bag of food flew out of my hand as I grabbed for my purse. At that time, female agents were permitted to carry our weapon and credentials in our purses, so I knew I had to protect these valuable items, as I did my own life. The man knocked me to the ground fighting hard to get the purse from me. We ended up rolling on the ground close to his car and then I heard another voice. "Get her in the car, get her in the car." At this point I had an immediate intuitive thought that these people were drug dealers and that they were going to kill me with my own weapon! As both men were picking me up and putting me in the back seat, I immediately cried out to God, "If you will but save me, I will serve you with my life!" At that I felt like some powerful force had come along and gave me supernatural strength to break the hold of these two men and to get away. As I made the break, the strap on my purse broke and I lost my purse, but at this point I was so grateful to be alive! Hearing my screaming, several people came out of the hotel to see what the ruckus was. I was so angry as I saw them all standing nearby watching me fight for my life yet not one person came to my aid!

When the local police arrived at the hotel they took my report and told me that they were detaining some people in the nearby vicinity and they wanted me to see if these were the people who assaulted me. They also told me that one of the bystanders was willing to be a witness as well. When I got into the patrol car with this individual, I noticed that he was a drunk who smelled awful and wore tattered clothes. He looked like a street bum. To my surprise, I think this man turned out to be a God-send or perhaps an angel unaware! I will never know until I get to heaven. He saw the whole assault take place and was able to identify the assailants. On the other hand, I was not so successful because I was just fighting for my life! When I saw the first person, I did not recognize "her!" Then they brought a second person and I did not recognize him either. Then they brought a third person and immediately I said, "That's him! That's him!" Later a police officer told me that the suspects had six crow bars on the floor of the passenger's side and all they would have had to do was hit me over the head and knock me out to get me into their car, but they did not! Did God prevent them from doing this? All I know is that God saved my life that night. The police found my purse and weapon under the front driver's seat.

He Was There All the Time

The police then told me the bizarre story of how the suspects were stopped. After assaulting me, they took off and drove down a nearby street with very wealthy homes. A truck had come down the street earlier that night and accidently dumped oil on the street, making it very messy, so a woman called the police to report it. While the police were investigating the situation, the call came over the radio that I had been mugged. When the car turned down that exact street, the police stopped it because it fit a description of a car they were looking for over another, earlier purse snatching. While checking the details, they heard of my incident and checked the car. Sure enough, they found my purse, gun and credentials. Unbelievable. Again, another God incident! When we went to court the three people were charged for drug dealing and assault of a federal officer and the case was won because of this hobo's testimony! I never even had to testify!!! I thanked him profusely and wanted to take him out to lunch with my attorney, but he refused the offer with his head hanging low. I do believe that God sends the most unexpected people into our lives when we need them the most. I had to repent of my critical attitude of him when I first met him. He turned out to be not only my life saver, but my hero.

Little did I know that someone else was praying for me that very night! Years later, I found out that on that same night, a man in New York City was praying that God would bring a godly woman into his life to marry! I believe that God kept me alive for a beautiful encounter that I would have years later.

On a humorous note, a funny thing happened to me one day while relaxing at the hotel poolside. A guy came up to me saying that he was from New York City and wanted to sell me some drugs! I could not believe my ears! He told me he was living out of his sports car and he was down south to strike up some drug deals. I thought to myself: if he only knew who I was and that I was in town working a big undercover drug case!! After I told him I was not interested, he never bothered me again.

Once my work down south was completed, I went back to my original home office to be put on another drug case. By this time, I was getting good at this undercover work! But this case was quite different and much scarier. It was an all office drug bust of big time drug dealers. Our plan was to go to several different homes very early in the morning and wake people up and then arrest them. The DEA (Drug Enforcement Agency), state police, and local police were all involved in this huge area-wide drug raid. The night before, I was told by the lead agent that I would be standing under the bedroom window of one of the suspects that we were going to arrest. I was with another agent who was holding a shotgun and I held the ammunition for him. I was given a bullet proof vest and told to get to the office in the wee hours of the morning because we were going to show up at his house before

He Was There All the Time

sunrise. I was ready! How very exciting to think this was like a TV drama only it was the real deal! Until I tried to sleep. During the night, I woke up in a cold sweat and fear started gripping my heart. I got on my knees and started to pray very hard for these drug busts that no one would be hurt. I prayed until peace came over me. By then it was time to go. We arrived at this huge fancy log home deep in the woods and we all quietly took our places waiting for further orders. The men at the front door knocked several times but got no answer. They then broke down the door and several people went inside thinking the man was in bed. When they got to his room they found the bed empty. They called all of us into the house to do a search, but he was nowhere to be found. What we did find shook me to the core. On his night stand were several loaded weapons from sawed off shotguns to handguns and those weapons were in front of the window – the very window we were standing below just minutes before! When the agents and police knocked down the man's door, his alarm went off and no one knew how to disarm it, so it kept on ringing very loudly. After a short period of time, the suspected drug dealer came driving up his driveway and heard his alarm sounding. He saw all the people around and thought they were the police responding to the alarm. We came to find out that his alarm was connected to the local police station so if it went off the police would come to his house and check it out. We also came to find out this man was an art dealer and had very valuable pieces of art in his home.

Therefore, he had an alarm connected to the police station, in case someone should break into his home.

Unbeknownst to him, this man walked peacefully into his own arrest. But what is even more amazing is what he told us. During the middle of the night, he and his common-law wife had a huge fight and she stormed out of the house and went to another alleged drug dealers house while he took off in his car! Could that be why the Lord woke me up in a cold sweat and told me to pray hard. I believe many lives were spared that day because of the Lord's divine intervention! Not one soul was injured, and many arrests were made that morning without incident.

During this time, my personal life got turned upside down in a way I never dreamed or imagined. I met a divorced man in my singles group at my Catholic Church and we hit it off immediately. It did not take long for me to get very close to him spiritually, emotionally and physically. As the weeks went by, I just knew I wanted to be with him every day. We had very deep open, heart-to-heart talks and we just clicked like two peas in a pod. I began spending more time at his house than at mine. We eventually talked about tying the knot in marriage and I was so close to saying yes but I was not at peace. I still had not resolved the issue of becoming a missionary! Was I to finally quit running from God and just become a nun and live out the plans I thought He had for me? I still felt like a fugitive running from God for fear of what He was asking of me. Crunch time came once again. The Bureau was transferring me, and I had to face the truth -- would I leave my job and marry him or continue to pursue this phantom dream of mine. As painful as it was, I told him I had to take the transfer.

NYC, Gotham, the Big Apple

Now for the big move to New York City! The thought of living in such a big city terrified me; however, I had a friend who lived there. It was the daughter of the woman I met at the meeting with my mom who first told us about the FBI. She helped me find an apartment in her complex. My introduction to the Big Apple was an eye opener. I was on a house hunting trip and this woman asked me to join her for dinner one night after work. We met in the city to go to a very nice restaurant but could not find a parking spot anywhere! We drove and drove and finally found one nearby; however, there was a time limitation. Foolish me said: "I bet nothing will happen. How will they ever find our car on this side street when there are so many other busy streets to be checked on!" My girlfriend did not share the same opinion. She told me that they were very strict about enforcing parking laws; however, she gave in to my idea because

He Was There All the Time

we had been driving for so long. We parked and went in for a wonderful meal.

After dinner, while talking, we started hearing this loud pounding on the roof and looked out a window to see that it had started raining very hard. It was a torrential downpour, so we decided we better get home. Fortunately, we were not parked very far away. However, when we got to the spot where we thought we had parked the car, it was not there! Then we became confused. Perhaps we did not park on this street, in this "particular spot." Getting soaked, we kept going around in circles trying to recall where we parked our car! Finally, she had the idea that she should call the police to see if our car was towed! Back in those days, you had to find a telephone booth on the street to make a call, so we kept walking until we found one. Sure enough, the car had been towed to the impound garage. I felt awful because it truly was my fault that this happened to us! She warned me, but I did not believe that the city could be as strict as she said they were. Next, we had to find a taxi to take us to the garage; however, we could not find one as everyone was scrambling around getting taxis in this rain storm. Finally, one came, and we arrived at the garage only to find out how much it cost to retrieve the car! Neither of us had enough money on us so my friend had to take another taxi home to get money and return. Oh, what a nightmare my first visit to NYC turned out to be!

Life got better for a while, once I moved there and got settled into my new job and new apartment. I lived on Staten Island and the ferry boat ride was a pleasure to look forward to each night. The sunset always was so beautiful, and despite the crowds, it was a very peaceful ride home after the rush of the day. However, it did not take long for me to discover that I had many unwanted friends living with me in my apartment -- huge roaches and a stray cat I took in to keep me company! At night, the cat would cry and cry, so I would let him into my bedroom to be with me. Then he would get into bed and bite me. I could not even get a restful night's sleep because of him and had to finally let him go. But the roaches were another story! They were not so willing to leave! They were everywhere, including my bathroom and the kitchen. Oftentimes I would open a drawer only to find one crawling around. I could not handle this. Despite the beautiful view I had of one of the bridges in NYC and the gorgeous sunsets, my home life was becoming a prison with which I could not live. Was God preparing me for the mission field, I thought?

During this time, I started dating an FBI agent who told me about another apartment in another part of the city that was vacant and perhaps I could move in there. Would life be better? I did not know but I was willing to find out, so I pursued it. Soon after I moved in, I found the problem still followed me. Those little creatures were everywhere and to make matters worse they were now in my

He Was There All the Time

bedroom and in bed with me! I woke up one night only to find a huge one crawling on my face! Enough was enough! I had to move again! This same friend recommended that I move into his friend's garage studio apartment about 2 ½ hours from the city. That meant a five hour commute every day. Which was the best of two evils? the commute or the roaches? I chose the commute. I would leave in the dark and come home in the dark every day and that was wearing on me physically and emotionally. I just kept thinking about my old boyfriend and wondering if I should just give up this crazy life and go back to him. We tried to keep it together, but it was just not working. We both started going out with other people. During this time, I also became very ill and suffered with horrible pain, both physically and emotionally. I knew my life was a mess!

To help relieve my stress, I bought a bike and would ride through the beautiful rolling hills outside the city. It was gorgeous, especially during the spring when all the leaves were budding and flowers blooming. One day, I pulled off a lonely densely wooded road and just sat by a quiet stream. I told the Lord how lonely I was and how I wished I had someone to share my life with and to do simple things like bike together. That conversation was soon forgotten by me but not to the Lord! Several months later the Lord sent me a wonderful companion and as we were biking together one day, I recalled my prayer on that lonely road and how the Lord does not forget those moments or the prayers we pray during those dark times in our lives! He is so good!

After many trips to the doctor, it was determined that I needed surgery for a cyst I had. There was no guarantee that this would take away the pain, but it was my last option. For months, I suffered and could barely keep myself together to take that long commute and work my job as well. But somehow God gave me the grace I needed to get through this very rough period in my life. I did not deserve His mercy because of the lifestyle I had been living but His love continued to call me forth into a deeper relationship with Him. I really felt that perhaps God was punishing me; however, I did not feel like God was abandoning or rejecting me.

One day while taking the train into NYC, I went from car to car trying desperately to find a seat because it was too long a train ride to stand in pain. Finally, I found a seat with two men beside me and two in front of me. I found it quite unnerving that the man in front of me kept looking up from a little book he was reading and smiling at me. Why would he smile at me and then return to his book, which looked like a small, pocketsize Bible. A little voice that I had gotten so accustomed to hearing in the past said, "Talk to him." I responded: "What am I to say to him?" All these other men were reading the New York Times and Wall Street Journal and I felt uncomfortable asking him what he was reading, so I kept silent. I said nothing and just gave a little yet painful smile when he smiled at me.

Finally, the train arrived at Grand Central Station and everyone quickly scrambled off, including this well-dressed businessman. I just sat there waiting for the crowd to diminish before leaving the train. Then I heard that still small voice again: "If you don't go looking for him you might never see him again!" I began arguing with myself: "Why does it matter? Am I going to marry him!?" But this time I jumped out of my seat and pushed my way through hundreds of people looking for this businessman who looked just like every other businessman going into the city! As I was pushing through what seemed a herd of cows, I asked myself: "What am I to say to him if I do find him?" But I received no answer. To my utter surprise, I stumbled onto him, so I tugged at his suit. He turned to me as I said nervously: "Sir, I was sitting across from you on the train and I was wondering, are you a Christian?" He then said, "Well, yes I am a Catholic Christian." I could not believe my ears. Then I told him I was new to the area and I was looking for a good church. Could he direct me to one and he said yes!

Because the crowd was pushing us, we could not talk so he suggested we go into the main terminal to talk. When we got into an open area, he asked for my address because he was in a hurry. He told me he would mail the information. It all happened so quickly I did not think until afterwards that I had just given a total stranger my address! How could I have been so foolish! I got scared and immediately went into prayer for protection for my impulsive stupidity! Well a few days later, the information did arrive but without leaving his name. I thought that was strange. Perhaps he was angel and not a real person. I took the information and made my way to this so-called church of sorts. It was not a church at all; it was a group of people who met in a gym of a Catholic High School for Sunday Mass. What kind of a group was this and why was I led here I thought? While living in New York City, I could never find the right church to worship in. I recall one time I went to the priest at one of the churches I was attending and asked if there was an adult singles group I could join. He rudely told me that this church was mainly made up of families and no singles. But I could join a local college group if I wanted to be with young, single people. That was not the answer. I was not looking for college kids who were much younger than me. I needed to meet some young adults who were single professionals like me. But where was I to go? I was desperate. I decided to give this strange group of believers a chance.

On my first visit, I stumbled into a bible study. I was asked how I found out about this small gathering of worshippers. I told them the story and they said they did not know of any such person matching the description I gave. Then it occurred to them that there was a gentleman who came very occasionally and perhaps

He Was There All the Time

it was him, but they could not be sure. Unfortunately, because I did not have his name, no one could verify who this "strange person" was or if he even existed.

I was made to feel very welcome among this small group of believers. I learned that the diocese was doing an experiment. They wanted to start a group that worshipped like the first followers of Jesus in the book of Acts. They met in people's homes for prayer, bible study, meals and fellowship. On Sundays, they met in this gym for bible study and the celebration of Mass. It was a "cool idea" I thought but still there were no single people there. It was mainly married couples with families. But the redeeming grace was that I was made to feel welcome. I started going to people's homes during the week for fellowship and I made some good friends.

Then it happened! A real God incident! I joined a home bible study and when I walked in, there was the man I thought I had met on the train! At first, I was not sure because it had been a couple of months since I first saw him, and he was never at Sunday Mass at the high school. When the other guests asked who I was and how I got there, I told them about this man I met on the train. I then asked him if he was that man and he said YES! I couldn't believe my ears. Not only was he a real person, he was the bible study teacher, as well. His name was Greg. The night went beautifully and as we conversed, I asked him why he kept smiling at me on the train. He told me that he always prayed for people on the train and that morning the Lord told him I was in deep pain (which I was but I did not think it showed) and that he was to pray for me. He also told me he was reading from his Gideon Bible and every few minutes he looked up to pray for me. As I continued to go to this weekly Bible study, I shared about my life and my need for prayer because I was suffering from severe pain and I needed surgery. I also asked this gentleman why he was never at church on Sundays and he said he had a home in the country that he was remodeling on weekends and he went to church there.

Another memory I recall where the Lord came to me in a very powerful way was the day I was terribly upset and frustrated about the pain I was experiencing, with no answer as to its cause. I called a friend who invited me to her home. I debated about going out because it was stormy outside, and I knew the desolate, country roads would be slick. I decided to go anyway. In my frustration, I sped around a corner on a winding road and lost control of my car. The next thing I saw was my car going off the road and up a steep, stony embankment. In my mind, I saw the car tipping over and landing upside down. The car was totally on its side and I knew I was heading for a crash on a road rarely traveled! But instead a miracle took place! I know beyond a shadow of a doubt that the Lord saw my state of mind and my broken heart and He sent angels to lift my car and put it on its four wheels safely on the road. Shaken up I tried to drive the car but realized I was not going very far due to two flat tires! I got to a place where I could make a call to AAA and to my friend to tell her I had just been in an accident. I know that day God kept me alive for a reason -- which was just around the corner.

After several weeks, the day of my surgery finally came. This small group of believers were there for me as if they were my family. But still I felt so all alone as I wrestled with God about my messed-up life and His will for me. I felt so depressed and lost at the time, so I told the Lord to take me home while on the operating table because I could not handle the deep pain or fear of letting go and letting God have His way with my life. I was afraid that if I surrendered my life fully to God, He would rob me of my dreams and ask me to serve Him as a nun. Oh, what anguish I had caused myself all those years because I was afraid to let go and trust God with my life. I still wanted to be in control and in trying to be in control, I was totally out of control because nothing was working out right in my life. I had no peace or joy, just miserable emptiness. The time to stop running from God like a fugitive was soon coming to a halt. But I was still not quite ready to totally let go.

The surgery went very well until I woke up in the recovery room. When I came to, I was freezing cold. When I realized I was still alive I began to scream. I didn't know which was worse -- freezing or knowing I was still alive and I had to face God and myself with all my internal pain. The nurses quickly came over to quiet me down and get me to my room where I recuperated over the next several days. During this time, I decided to talk to a priest about my dilemma and one was sent to me. I told him that if God wants me to be a nun I will do it and I asked if he could help me. He told me he could help me and that he would be back to talk further. I was in the hospital about a week however he never came back. I was really upset because finally I was making headway and when I asked for help, the help never came back! I prayed very hard asking God what He wanted me to do with my messed-up life. I told Him I was finally ready to totally surrender and do whatever He wanted with me. I then asked Him, "Do you want me to (A) go back to my old boyfriend, (B), (C) or (D) naming three different religious orders." I then heard His still small voice say, "Did you ever think there was an E?" I replied "an E? What do you mean?" But He did not say. He was totally silent on what "E" meant. I felt like a ton of weight just dropped off my shoulders and heart that day. I was finally able and ready to let go and do whatever the Lord had in mind and I had inner peace for the first time in years! I felt scared and excited at the same time. What could God possibly have in mind for me? I tried hard to figure it out, but I really had no idea! I just waited on Him to guide me.

I recalled a moment in time when I was living in the roach infested house and I was ready to quit my job and leave NYC. I was riding the bus into the city that day and again heard my Lord's still small voice: "Do not give up. If you do, you will never know the plans I have for you." Was that God or my dad speaking to me or perhaps both? Now here I was in a hospital bed in NYC and He was telling me He had a very special plan, "E." Even though I did not know what it was, I was very glad I did not give up that day on the bus and that God was not giving up on me even though I had asked Him to take me home to be with Him.

While in the hospital, friends came to visit but the most special visit was a "phone visit" from Greg. He told me that he was on vacation with his two children and could not come see me, but that I was in his prayers. I learned that he was divorced.

When I went home, my mom came to stay with me but begged me to "come home" to my parents' house so that she could better care for me over the next six weeks of recuperation. Reluctantly, I went home and continued to pray intensely to the Lord about my future. I prayed a novena to the Blessed Mother which would end on August 15th, the feast of Our Lady's Assumption. I begged the Lord to please give me His answer by the end of the novena and He did -- but not in the way I expected. During this time, I called a priest I knew who was trying to help me with my discerning process. I told him about my experience in the hospital and that I really felt God was calling me to the order with which he was affiliated, but I had no peace. He said I probably was scared to leave my secure job and step into the unknown. He then told me that he was going to be in my area doing a retreat in about a month and we could talk about it face to face. On the last day of the novena, I felt I heard the Lord say that I was not to join the order that this priest was affiliated, or any other order. Instead I was to marry Greg! I was shocked because he was divorced, and I hardly knew him! This could not be God telling me this and again I was in anguish over this; but at the deepest level in my being, I had total peace. On the surface, I was very anxious and arguing with myself that it was just me and not God but at a deeper level, I had this crazy internal peace. How could this be, I thought? He was a Wall street executive and I still had a burning passion to be a missionary. It was so strange that I could feel such conflict and peace at the same time. It was like the feeling I had when the FBI came into my life. I did not go looking for either of these situations, yet I had peace about each one, when nothing made sense to me! Could this be the "E" that God told me about in the hospital? I thought how could I think such irrational thoughts when I knew nothing about this man. Did he have a girlfriend and how could God love and accept me if I was to marry a divorced man when I knew divorce was wrong. The church is adamant when it comes to divorce and remarriage. Would I have to leave the church then? Again, all these questions tore at my heart, but I still had peace! Was it false peace just to appease my heart's desire or could I possibly be hearing from God. Years later I learned that God sometimes allows imperfect things to happen in our lives for His greater glory. Perhaps it's not His perfect will but if we give our lives to Him, He can use it all for His eternal purposes. Perhaps God does write straight with crooked lines. Time would tell.

One night while resting at my parents' house, I got a very unexpected phone call. A few people from my little Bible study group knew that I had gone home to my parent's house for six weeks, so I thought it was one of them. But no! It was Greg! I asked how he got my number and he told me he was trying to contact me in NYC and when I did not answer, he asked one of our friends where I was. We had such a sweet conversation and when it was time to say good bye he asked if he could call me again. I was quick to say sure!

For the next several weeks we carried on a lovely relationship by phone and I could not help wondering why he was calling me? When the time came for me to return to NYC, he asked if I would like to go on a date with him. I was floored! He told me that a friend of his owned a yacht and he wanted to take me for a ride on the harbor. Oh, how exciting, I thought. I had one request, however. My youngest sister and her best friend were planning to come back with me for a mini-vacation, so they would be with me. I asked if they could join us and he readily agreed.

The yacht was huge, and my sister and her girlfriend stayed in the aft while Greg and I stayed forward and talked and talked for hours. We probably spent eight or more hours on that boat just sharing our life stories, and by the end of the night, I just knew I had heard correctly. This man was exactly right for me. When we returned home that night my sister and her girlfriend said: "We just know you are going to marry this man. He is just so right for you". I could not believe what I was hearing because they did not know him at all! How could they know what I thought I heard from the Lord after praying my novena? I had not told a soul about my prayer and what I felt the Lord told me.

During this time in my life, I wanted to know Jesus in a very intimate personal way and I told Him I did not care the cost. With my ongoing conversations with Greg, I came to find out he had what I was looking for. I loved the fact that out of his brokenness, woundedness, and neediness, he came to know Jesus in a very deep and personal way. They conversed as best friends. He told me that I could have the same thing if I asked Jesus to be my personal Lord and Savior and let Him (not me) be the boss of my life. He talked to the Lord about everything! His faith was so childlike and trusting. I saw such love and peace and joy flow from him and I wanted what he had. One day, I courageously did just that. I asked Jesus to be my Lord and Savior as well. As Greg and I got talking more and more about our lives, he told me that he did not believe an annulment was right for him because he went into his first marriage with the full intention that it would work. He blamed himself for its failure and that is what led to his conversion and personal relationship with Jesus. Instead, he asked the Lord for forgiveness, healing and a second chance at marriage. His prayer was that he would do it God's way and make amends for the way he failed the first time. He prayed this prayer in his apartment on Sunday February 14th, the night I was mugged! Little did he know what God had in mind three years later! In this very sweet humble man, I could see, feel and touch the merciful heart of Jesus. God brought two very broken souls together to glorify Him with a new beginning. Greg used to tell me to just keep my heart's eyes fixed on Jesus on the cross (and not man) and to follow Him no matter the cost and He would take care of everything else.

The next few weeks flew by and they were wonderful just being with this man. We just bonded tightly, and I did not know why. Then I could not keep it a secret anymore. I had to tell him what I believed the Lord spoke to my heart at the end of my novena. We decided to get together one night after work. I nervously went to his condo and just stared at him. He then said, "I have something to share with you too." I became very nervous and thought perhaps he wanted to stop seeing me for some reason that he was about to disclose. We went back and forth as to who was going to share their well-kept secret first. I feared I had not heard from the Lord and was about to find that out, so I begged him to share his secret first and he finally consented. He said that the Lord had spoken to his heart that he was to marry me!!! I was shocked because we had only been out on a few dates so how could he know? I then confessed what the Lord had spoken to my heart at the end of my novena. I had even journaled it, so he knew I was telling him the way it really happened. We both rejoiced over this wonderful news.

At about this time, my family was preparing a surprise toga party for my dad's birthday and I thought that this would be a good time to bring Greg home to meet my parents and my siblings. He agreed to it and we stayed at a friend's home until the night of the party. It was a wild party because we all had to dress up in togas. What a way to meet your future in-laws. We had a fabulous time that weekend and when it was time to return to NYC dad brought Greg and I to the airport. As we said our good-byes, dad gave Greg a big bear hug and told him to "take good care of his little girl" and Greg assured him he would. Despite his being divorced, I took this comment to mean that Greg was accepted by dad (and hopefully mom too.)

When we got back to NYC, Greg took me out for dinner one night to a lovely restaurant and popped the question! He said, "Cheryl I would like to marry you." Nervously I said yes! Then I asked him when do you want to set the date and he jokingly replied, "by the end of this year so I can include you as a tax write off." Knowing nothing about taxes I naively thought that I would be saving him a lot of money only to find out later he did this because he feared I would break off our engagement and run away like I had done before with others. Now mind you, it was October when he popped the question, so we did not have much time to prepare for our wedding.

Also during this time, I met with the priest from the religious community I was thinking of joining. I told him what had transpired in my life and he was not happy to hear of my news at all. I literally got very sick right on the spot in the restaurant where we met. I thought to myself he must be right because he is a priest and he represents the whole Catholic Church. It didn't matter if I thought I had God's blessing and peace. I must be wrong in thinking I heard from God. As we parted his last words to me were "there is a narrow way and a wide way." I never said a word to him but as I left I thought to myself I believe in my heart that I have heard from the Lord and although none of this makes sense, I believe I had chosen the narrow way. As I turned away I thought to myself I am about to walk away from the Catholic Church but not from God and I will go forward and once again just "do it afraid."

The next step was to tell mom and dad. Of course, they wondered why the rush. Mom tried hard to convince me to wait until the next summer, but I told her I wanted a very simple wedding at home at Christmas, because it was a special time of year for me. Mom wanted us to have a very fancy, formal wedding but I wanted it to be very small and intimate. Greg and I also talked about washing each other's feet as part of our ceremony, symbolizing our commitment to love and serve each other in all humility until death do us part. Little did I know then what this simple gesture of dedication, devotion and love would mean. I still could not believe the grace I received from my parents in their acceptance of Greg. They just loved him. Dad even said he had a good friend who was a Protestant minister who could probably marry us. We met with this pastor on several occasions for marital counseling and he too came to the same conclusion that God truly brought us together for His purposes and glory.

Next came the ordering of wedding invitations, as well as the finding a caterer who could do our wedding reception on such short notice. But God blessed us with the most beautiful invitations and a great caterer. My dream was to wear my mom's wedding gown, and except for a few alterations, the gown fit beautifully. With the help of the Lord, Greg and I wrote out our own wedding vows. The day of our wedding the area was hit with a huge blizzard and all our out of town guests arrived at my parent's home just as the airport was shutting down. How beautiful it was to look out the window and see the snow falling softly as we

He Was There All the Time

exchanged our wedding vows and washed each other's feet. We truly felt the Lord's presence and blessing on this- Our Wedding Night.

Marriage, Bible School & Family

Our first year of marriage was like a continuous, glorious honeymoon. Greg continued working as an executive and I continued my career with the FBI. About six months into our marriage, however, Greg mentioned to me one day that he wanted to leave his Wall Street job and go to bible school so that we could serve the Lord in full time ministry. I could not have agreed more! I was so excited that I could hardly contain my emotions. Little did I ever dream when I said yes to God and to Greg that we would go into ministry for the Lord! Then began the search for a good bible school. Unfortunately, we were met with great obstacles when some schools discovered that we were Catholic, and that Greg was divorced. I felt like we were lepers looking in from the outside, rejected because of our backgrounds. But this did not discourage Greg. He really believed that God had a place for us and sure enough He did! We called the minister who had married us, and he told us about his wonderful bible school. We sent for literature and were incredibly blessed when we found out that not only did they accept Catholics but divorced Catholics, as well. It was at this bible school that we grew in our faith and experienced the mercy and healing love of God in new and freeing ways. He truly is the God of second chances! In fact, we found out after we arrived that half of the student population was from a Catholic background!

Within six months of the date we applied, we sold our condo in one day and were heading off to a new adventure! We grew by leaps and bounds that first year of bible school. One day, while walking to school for classes, I mustered up the courage to ask Greg what kind of ministry he wanted to go into. He told me he wanted to be a pastor and I knew he would make a great one. However, my desires were not met with the same enthusiasm. When I mentioned that my life-long dream was to be an overseas missionary, he said, "No way!" He desired a clean bed and hot shower and working in a poor country would not provide those amenities. I remember being very sad that day and wondering if I had made a mistake in marrying him. Perhaps that priest was right, and I had chosen the wrong road. After much tears and prayers, I decided to let go and surrender my heart's desire to God and I prayed that His will, not mine be done! After a lifetime of hope, I finally let go of this dream and for the first time in years, felt so free and peaceful inside. This surrender brought sunshine into my disheartened soul and I felt like a ton of bricks had been lifted off my heart that day. I never told Greg what I had done. I just left the whole situation up to God and let Him decide what was best for us. After all, He did bring us together for His purposes and not mine or Greg's.

Soon after something quite strange happened to my husband. We had bought a computer to write our papers and for relaxation Greg had bought a flight simulator game to play in his down time. He really got into that game so much that he decided to start taking flying lessons at the local airport. But the next question was: what was he going to do with all this experience? After all, we went to bible college to grow in our faith and to serve the Lord in fulltime ministry. How did all this fit together? After much prayer, Greg felt that the Lord was calling him to be an overseas missionary pilot! Again, I could not believe my ears. When I totally let go, God took over in a way that I would never have dreamt or imagined. Unfortunately, our lives did not go the way we thought they were going to go. Once Greg got his private license, he went on for his instrument rating because he knew he would need this if he were to fly in all kinds of weather and terrain. During this time, we had so much fun flying together as he got in his required hours. My dad was a pilot, as well, and he and Greg often flew together. That was quality time for them and it drew them quite close.

He Was There All the Time

Then something very unusual happened in our second year at the bible school. One day one of the administrators called Greg and said he needed to talk to him. At first, we were concerned. Had we done something wrong and they were now going to ask us to leave bible school? We went to prayer regarding this meeting that Greg was to have. While he was in the meeting, I sat in the car waiting for him. The Lord once again spoke to my heart that I was not to be afraid but that they were going to ask Greg to come on staff at the school. I could not believe what I was hearing from the Lord. When Greg left this meeting, he came to the car with a shocked look on his face. He went on to tell me that the school offered him a job on staff just like the Lord told me minutes before! With that, another adventure began. Because of Greg's executive business background, the school felt he would be a real asset and, sure enough, he was. The school was in the red and under Greg's guidance and wisdom, it moved into the black.

During our second year at bible school, the Lord blessed us with our first child, a beautiful baby girl. I loved being a first-time mom. Unfortunately, however, she was not getting enough milk from me when I nursed her. I felt like a failure and blamed myself for her lack of nutrition. Yet my wonderful woman doctor, came up with an agreeable solution. I would nurse my daughter and then bottle feed her until her needs were met. Soon after she was a very happy, peaceful child. I thanked the Lord for sending me such a good and wise woman to be my doctor. Not only did I have a hard time with nursing, but I also experienced another difficulty. After coming off my high from giving birth to this beautiful child, I slipped into the baby blues – *postpartum depression*. I would become very agitated over stupid things and would start crying for no reason at all. I recall having a minor tiff with my husband and blasting him for it as if he had committed an unpardonable sin! I knew then I had to make another visit to my doctor. She assured me that this hormonal imbalance was quite common after giving birth but that it would pass and eventually it did! How happy I was to be back to my normal self again so that I could truly enjoy caring for my little baby girl.

As life settled down, I started thinking about going back to school to become a social worker to help supplement our income. However, the nearest school was over an hour away from our home. I sent for the syllabus and when I read it, I could not agree with everything they taught so I let this idea go. I knew I had lost my teaching license, so I needed to find another program and I loved helping people, so I thought social work would be a good choice. But for some strange reason this door seemed to be closing. Then Greg suggested that I call the state education department to confirm for sure that I had lost my teaching license. I recalled what my principal had told me when I left my teaching job to join the FBI. She told me that unless I had two years of experience as a remedial reading specialist, I would not be permanently certified and that I was throwing away my Master's Degree. She felt that all the hard work I had put into the degree would be going down the drain if I left teaching for the FBI. Perhaps I had made a huge mistake like she said and now it was coming back to haunt me! I knew I was right, but I humbly decided to call the education department just to appease my husband. When I told the woman my situation, she said that the regulations had changed since the time I had taught school. She said that my experience as a classroom teacher could be applied toward my permanent certification! I told her that I had taught in a regular classroom for several years. All she had to do was confirm this fact and I would receive my permanent certification. I could not believe what I was hearing. I thought to myself that once again, God was looking out for me and this truly was another one of His God incidences. Nothing less than a miracle! But what she said next really convinced me that this was God's intervention coming to me through my husband. It was July when I called the education office and she said that even though this had been the regulation for the last several years, the department was returning to the original requirements (which was to teach two years as a reading specialist). That change was to occur in the next month. If I wanted to be certified, I had to do it right away before the new regulations went into effect. I quickly complied and put all the information together that was needed, and within a short period of time, I had my permanent certification to teach both in the regular classroom and as a reading specialist.

When I look back, I see that it truly was God working in a quiet mysterious way in my life. Why? Because I was very happy being a full-time mom. I had no real desire to work outside the home at that time, so why was I even thinking of going back to school? Yet, I see how God was using this situation to get my attention. He really wanted me to obtain my permanent certification before the change occurred and he used my husband to encourage me to make that call to the education department. I was convinced I was no longer certified and with only a month left, I would not have been. The timing of this event was surreal. God once again worked in a very strange and mysterious way to get my attention. Little did I know how important this decision was going to play out later in my life. Nothing is ever wasted with God. His timing and ways are perfect if only we are listening and obeying what He says.

My daughter was born in July and that following year I had another strange encounter with the Lord. It was Good Friday and it was during the 12:00 noon to 3:00 PM time frame when I experienced a potential loss. Despite the heavy rain, I needed to do some last-minute shopping for Easter Dinner, so I invited a little friend to join us to help me with my daughter. My little 8-year old friend loved being a mother's helper. She adored my baby girl. While driving,

He Was There All the Time

I told her that I needed to make two stops. First, we would go to the supermarket and do some shopping. After that, we would go to the drugstore which was at the very end of the big supermarket plaza. I thought I had made my plans very clear to her and never gave it a second thought. By the time we got to the store, it was raining so hard that I decided cautiously, to drop her and my 8-month old baby off in front of the supermarket door. I told her to quickly go inside and get a basket, while I parked the car. Once parked, I went inside but did not see the little girl or my daughter anywhere. It had only been a few short minutes. Where could she be, I thought. I told her exactly what to do. Did she decide to go down an aisle? Did someone talk to her and coax her to come with them? Fear gripped my pounding heart as I hurriedly rushed down each aisle to find them. Nowhere were they to be found. After canvassing the whole store, a couple of times, I went to a cashier who was stationed near the door and asked if she had seen a little girl with a baby? During this time, my mind went immediately went back to mother Mary when she lost Jesus in Jerusalem. I knew she felt the same kind of panic I felt so I prayed to her and Jesus for help. I also knew that she was right by His side at that very afternoon hour watching her son die a horrible death for me. Who better could I go to comfort me in my despairing moments. The timing of this event put me so close to Jesus and Mary and their suffering. Soon other people were helping me try to find the two children but to no avail. I could not believe how irresponsible I was to just leave two small children together without adult supervision. As we were getting ready to call the police, a customer asked if they could be in the drug store. I said no because I dropped them off in front of the supermarket door and I told the eight-year old to go in and get a basket. Being a seasoned parent, she said before you call the police let's go check out the drug store. She went to the drug store and found the little girl and my baby in a cart waiting by the front door! She then brought them both safely back to me. When I asked the little girl why she went outside in the pouring rain to the drug store she said she thought I said we were going there first and wondered why I had dropped them off in front of the supermarket! She figured she was supposed to get a cart and walk in the rain to the drug store. I learned a very hard lesson that day. Children don't always hear correctly what you say and never leave a baby with a small child. Believe me, it never happened again.

As part of our outreach ministry, Greg and I became involved in a ministry to unwed mothers. We were monthly weekend respite house-parents to a home for unwed moms. During this time, we met some wonderful moms who struggled with whether they should keep their babies or give them up for adoption. We had the privilege of being a listening ear as they shared their personal stories with us. Some were very heart wrenching, like one woman who had been a heavy drinker before coming to the home. When

He Was There All the Time

it came time to have her baby, she gave birth six weeks early to a tiny premature, sick baby girl. Her baby was born with Fetal Alcohol Syndrome. She decided that it was in the best interest of her baby to give her to two parents who could love and care for her. When we learned about this situation, Greg said, "why don't we adopt her?" While at Bible school Greg had gotten involved with a group of people from our school who would stand in front of abortion clinics and lovingly share reasons with women as to why they should keep their babies instead of aborting them. On a few occasions, Greg and the others would be arrested and taken to jail for standing up for God, truth and righteousness. He saw those times in jail as opportunities to minister to the other inmates who would ask him as to why he was there! He was always serving the Lord no matter what circumstance he found himself in! He said to me that if I can stand in front of abortion clinics and tell a woman why she should save her baby then we need to take the next step and help one of these women out by adopting her child and loving the baby. I could not have agreed more heartily. I then recalled the dream I had as a twelve-year old child. I wanted to be happily married, with children of my own. I also wanted to adopt children with special needs and now God was giving us the opportunity to do just that so how could I say no! When starting the process of adoption, however, we found out I was pregnant with our second child! Those were rough months. But we felt that if God was to give us this precious child, we would receive her with joy and trust Him for the strength to carry out His will.

When we heard about this very sick little baby, we were getting ready to go on a retreat with our bible college. We brought this prayer petition with us and asked the faculty and administrators to please pray with us during the few days we were together. I was to call social services and see if we had a chance to adopt her. The lady told me that there were three other couples before us that also had showed an interest in adopting this baby and that I was to get back to her in a few days. When I called her back, she told me that things did not work out for the other families and our name was next on the list. I was so excited and nervous that something happened to me that day. I started experiencing excruciating stomach pain that would not let up. As a young girl, I would have bouts of stomach problems, especially when I felt stressed, but they would come and go. This time the pain was not letting up and I got concerned. The pain made it very hard for me to think clearly and function. I just wanted to cry because of the intensity of the pain. After going to different doctors, and going for various tests, nothing showed up, so I just learned to cope as best as possible. But in the days and months ahead, it only got worse. Despite my ill health, we still went forward with the adoption. As the adoption process moved forward, I received a call one day from Social Services saying that the state was not going to release the baby to the Christian adoption agency with which we were working. When asked why, the woman would not give me a clear answer. Again, we had everyone at the bible school praying hard that God would open the door and remove all obstacles -- and sure enough He did!

We called our precious little one "our miracle baby" because she was born weighing a little over three pounds. She was in the hospital for about a month until she gained enough weight and strength to enter foster care. During this time, a background check had to be performed on us before the adoption agency could release her to us. After three months, she was finally home with us, but very sick. She had severe tremors and her little body would shake uncontrollably. She would scream for hours and hours. The only way we could help her was to keep her in her car seat with blankets tucked in tightly beside her to keep her body from thrashing around. Then we would put her pacifier in her mouth and wrap it around her head with a cloth so that when her head would shake it would not come out. But it invariably did come out and the screaming would continue. We tried other ways to calm her down; rocking her or holding her but nothing seemed to work.

She was also born with severe strabismus in both of her eyes and had to go for surgery to correct her vision. As she got older, she had to wear very thick glasses which she hated and continually tried ripping off her eyes. She also was born with deafness in one of her ears and partial deafness in the other ear. She was fitted for hearing aids which she would pull out of her ears because she hated them too. By the time she was six months old, she was placed in a special school that worked with her fine motor skills along with many other needed skills as well. As time went on, our little girl was becoming more and more delayed, so the schooling helped her to keep progressing in all facets of her life. She also was continually in and out of the hospital due to breathing problems and asthma. Her weakened immune system was badly compromised because of the fetal alcohol syndrome. However, God did miraculously heal the deafness in one of her ears.

During her first months with us, Greg and I took two-hour shifts at night, caring for her. Being pregnant and in lots of chronic pain, I was exhausted -- as was he -- because he still had to work every day. We also had an 18-month old child, who needed our loving care and attention, as well. After two months of total exhaustion, we decided to take our daughter to church and have our pastor lay hands on her and pray for her. After that prayer, she seemed to calm down considerably and we each got much needed rest.

Being Director of Development at the bible college required a lot of traveling for my husband, visiting contributors and raising financial support for the school. Although it was very hard not having him home during the week, we still managed to get by...until Monday, April 24th, my due date. I asked him to please

He Was There All the Time

cancel his appointments for that week; Greg responded that our first daughter was two weeks overdue and the doctors had to induce me. He was not too concerned that my due date was upon us. He promised that if I was to go into labor, he was only a few hours away and he would get home just in time for our baby's birth. I was very upset with him -- to say the least -- and yet, he was right. What if he stayed around for that week and nothing happened. It would have been a waste of time "just waiting."

Wouldn't you know it, Murphy's Law kicked in the very day that he left. Unlike my first delivery, I went into labor very quickly and four hours later a beautiful baby girl was born! With my first child, I was 23½ hours in labor. Because the umbilical chord was wrapped around her neck, the doctors had to be very careful with her delivery. But with my second child, she was ready to see the world as quickly as possible. Oh, how upset I was with my husband that he did not listen to me and stay home: "just in case." When his secretary called and told him I was in labor, he immediately rushed to the hospital. He arrived at the hospital just in the nick of time to see her born. Our little girl was a very easy-going baby. She had a very happy, pleasant personality even from the time of her infancy. She smiled a lot. She was born a few months after we adopted our second child and when we put the two babies aside each other, they were almost the same size!

One Sunday, we brought the two babies to the infant nursery at church, while we attended an evening service. Later that night, we received a call informing us that another baby had contracted the Respiratory Syncytial Virus (RSV) and was critically ill in the hospital. We were advised to keep a close watch on our babies. We feared our daughters might have been infected as well. Sure enough, the next day our adopted child came down with identical symptoms and had to be rushed to the hospital. During her week-long stay, she was kept in an oxygen tent to help with her breathing. Oftentimes the nurse would try to feed her milk, but she would spit it up. However, after a week, the hospital decided to release her, thinking that she was ready to come home. I did not feel she was ready at all, but the doctors insisted that she was stable enough to go home; the situation, however, only worsened and within a few days, she was back in the hospital.

Once stabilized, she was sent home, but she would clamp her lips real tight and refuse to drink her milk. She was only six months old but very strong willed! When my husband was in town working from his office, he would take over feeding duty when he got home at night. He would say to her "you will eat" and he would make her open her mouth, so she would drink her milk. Sometimes he was successful and other times she would spit it out. We had tried different formulas and it was always the same result. We were told it was not uncommon for babies born with fetal alcohol syndrome to have "failure to thrive" behaviors as she was displaying. But again, she was only 6 months old! How could she be that smart to try to starve herself and refuse to thrive. But we were seeing it for ourselves! Finally, after several visits to the doctor and back to the hospital, a decision was made that a feeding tube would be placed in her if she continued to refuse to eat after six weeks. My husband and I prayed hard that she would not have to succumb to that and just before we were to go to the hospital to have the tube emplaced, our daughter miraculously began to eat as if nothing was ever wrong!

While all of this was going on, Greg continued to work his long hours at the bible school, helping to raise funds which could keep it in the black. After this mission was accomplished, he came to me one day and said that it was time to pursue our missionary dream. I could not have agreed more. The school was saddened to see him go but the leadership also realized that God had other plans for us; however, we had one more obstacle to overcome. Greg needed to get his mechanics license to be an overseas missionary pilot. He had to be able to fix his own plane when it broke down. At this point, we did not have the money for him to do this and he needed to be working so that he could support our growing family. Once again, we went to prayer, asking the Lord for another miracle. Greg talked with the people at the airport where he was taking lessons to get their feedback. They had a mechanics department, but they could not afford to hire him as an apprentice. However, they knew of a larger airport nearby that might be willing to take Greg on as an apprentice and give him a salary. When this other airport heard about our plans to be missionaries, they readily agreed to hire him! Wow another miracle! It was not much of a salary but enough to pay our bills and stay afloat. With God's help, all our needs were met in ways we never dreamed or imagined.

When we were getting ready to move, we prayed as to where we should live. We decided that we wanted to live between both airports. Greg was going to continue his flight training at the one airport while getting his mechanics license at the other airport. There was a quaint little town which we both loved that was next to one of the airports. One day, Greg said that he would babysit the kids while I went house hunting. I prayed hard as I went through the newspaper in that little town and nothing showed up that was in our price range and had what we needed except for one house. I decided to go look for the house and when I saw it, I thought this is it! It was painted yellow (my favorite color) and it was very large and just down the street from one of the airports. I inquired of the owner as to the price and it was exactly what we could afford. Then came the tour. The home was in pristine shape with gorgeous curtains that would remain and elegant wall paper in most of the rooms. I questioned why they were renting such a

He Was There All the Time

beautiful home and the gentleman said that it had been his wife's home before they got married. However, they had just bought a new home of their own and she wanted to keep her old home and rent it out. Ironically, we were doing the same thing with the home Greg had fixed up before we got married. Greg and I once again said that the hand of God was on this move as one obstacle after another was removed.

Preparing for the Mission Field

One day, while doing laundry in the basement of our "new home," I heard out of the blue, that still small voice speaking to my heart again. The voice said: "I want to bless you and you can either accept the blessing or reject it." I said: "Lord I want to accept it" and He told me that He wanted to bless us with another child. I argued with Him that my health was horrible, and I could hardly take care of the three children we had. But I did not want to reject His gift, so I said: "Thy will be done." Then I had to tell my husband what had happened to me that day. I was very nervous that he would have thought I was crazy but quite the contrary! He told me that if God wants to bless us in this way he too was totally open to this wonderful gift from God. That very night our little gift from God was conceived. That was November 11th.

A week later my good friend who lived over 8 hours away had invited the three girls and I to come visit her for about a week. I had never driven that far alone before, especially with three little girls under the age of three! Greg had to work so he could not join us, but he encouraged me, telling me I could do it, so I went. While with my friend, I shared with her what happened in the basement and I asked if she could help me find out if I was truly pregnant. She said she would take me to a pro-life clinic and have me tested. When the woman asked if I wanted to be pregnant I told her yes, with great enthusiasm. She then said that the test was very faint as if I had just conceived but she thought for sure it was positive. I then told her what happened and we all rejoiced over this wonderful news.

About a month before this event occurred, I was at the park with my children. While they were having fun on the swings and the slide, something very strange happened in my heart. I felt like the Lord was gently and quietly asking me if I would give my heart more fully to Him and make Him truly number one before my husband, children and self. I also felt Him asking me if I would be willing to follow Him no matter the cost. I was scared as to what He was asking of me for fear that my husband or one of my children might die. My fears tried to overtake me that day in the park, but I said rather nervously, "Yes, Lord. Thy will be done. My family is not my own. They belong to you and so do I, so whatever you decide to do with us, we are yours to do with as you will." It was a very heavy day for me because I knew the Lord was asking for my all and He wanted to be number one in my life above all my hopes, dreams, and family. Once again, I let go in total surrender. But I must admit I "did it afraid" not knowing what lie ahead. That park holds a very special place in my heart. The slide had multi colored sides, so my daughter called it puzzle slide. That day as I looked at that slide, I thought my life was very much like it. I never knew what piece God was going to put into it next. Sometimes it was a bright colorful lovely piece and other times it was dark and heavy looking. That day I feared He was about to put a heavy piece in place, but I said whatever is next, Lord, thy will be done, and I meant it. Soon after this incident, is when He asked me if I would accept His gift of love into our family.

Although I suffered with a lot of physical pain during my third pregnancy, I was thrilled to be carrying a precious baby inside me. It was the weekend of Palm Sunday and we attended an airmen's family retreat in the mountains. We stayed in a very rugged, rustic, log cabin; not the best of places to stay. We made the best of it, however, and still had lots of fun. It was a great way to prepare for Easter. We had much to rejoice about. Life was good, so very good...until Good Friday. This was about to be another Good Friday trial identifying with my Lord in His suffering.

Our special needs daughter, who was two years old at the time, woke up very agitated and would not stop crying. I did everything I could to calm her down and finally she fell asleep for a nap.

He Was There All the Time

When she woke up she started crying real hard again. When getting out of her bunkbed, she fell to the floor. I thought she was playing around but I soon realized she was in pain and could not tell me what was wrong. Her speech and vocal skills were severely delayed, so I had to think for her. I called my husband and told him what was going on and he said take her to the doctors immediately. I called the doctor's office and they said come right in. When the doctor examined her, she could barely stand up on the table. Her little legs kept sinking down and she would collapse in pain. He then said get her to children's hospital immediately, which I did.

We waited anxiously as the doctors examined her tiny, frail body. As she lay there, her body got weaker and weaker and the doctors decided to keep her overnight. By now it was late in the evening and my husband showed up at the hospital, insisting that I go home and rest because I was about four months pregnant. He assured me that he would stay by her bedside the whole night. The next morning, before dawn, I was awakened by a phone call from Greg, saying our baby girl was totally paralyzed and dying! She was immediately placed into intensive care and fitted with a respirator. When I arrived at the hospital, I asked Greg what happened. He told me that about five in the morning, he heard her gasping for air and it awakened him out of sleep. He immediately called the nurse who got her hooked up to a breathing machine. By this time, they knew they were dealing with something very serious, so they brought in a neurologist. He said it appeared to him to be Guillain-Barre Syndrome, which could be brought on by a tick bite! He asked if we had been anywhere recently where she could have gotten bit by a tick. We told him that we had just spent that past weekend in the mountains at a retreat and stayed in a rustic, log cabin. He looked for the tick, but none could be found; however, he could find no other reason as to why she was totally paralyzed and in a coma.

Day after day, I would sit by her bedside and wonder if she would ever come out of her coma and be herself again. As I walked into the intensive care unit, there were pictures of many children who had been cared for there. Many had lived but several had died. I wondered which way our daughter was going to go. Our pastor came and prayed for her and he encouraged us to believe that God was going to heal her by Pentecost Sunday. He believed she would be running down the aisle at church. That gave us such hope. Even though she was unconscious, he told me to keep reading to her from her favorite Bible story book for children because she could still hear me. Every day I would sing little songs about Jesus's love for her and read her favorite stories to her. After a few weeks, no change was occurring in her condition, so the doctor suggested that they do a full blood transfusion: take all her blood out of her, purify it and return it to her. The danger was that someone else's blood had to be placed into her body to get the process started. The doctor was concerned that she might not pull through. He left this very difficult decision for Greg and me to think about. We prayed hard and decided to trust God with the results. We went forward with the doctor's recommendation. Soon after the transfusion, we started to notice some movement in her face, especially around her mouth. The nurse told me that she was trying to communicate. She said that when talking to our little girl, ask her questions and then ask her to open her mouth if the answer was yes. I did just that. I said: "Honey, Jesus wants to heal you just like He did Jairus' daughter. Do you want to be healed?" I then asked her if she would like to ask Jesus into her heart to be her Lord and Savior and to my wonderful surprise this little baby opened her tiny mouth just a little to tell me yes! I told her I would say a little prayer inviting Jesus to come into her heart and if she agreed with the prayer to open her mouth again and she did! Within a few days, her eyes opened, and she began to move her little body. She was in the hospital about a month and I know this situation had an effect on our other little girls who stayed with my brother and his family during this time.

When our little girl was finally released from the hospital, she had to learn how to eat, walk and talk all over again. As delayed as she was, she was now even further delayed and had to go to physical and occupational therapy for several weeks. After this horrific event, I wondered if this is what the Lord was preparing me for when I had that encounter with Him a few months prior in the park at puzzle slide. Little did I know what lie ahead. The rest of my pregnancy was uneventful, and a beautiful baby boy was born to us a few months later.

During this time, we did run into some financial stress. Our van was not working very well, and it needed major repairs which we could not afford. I was sharing this concern with my good friend, (who lived eight hours away) asking her to pray with us for an answer as to what to do. Unbeknown to me, she and her husband prayed about buying us a new used van! To our surprise she and her husband drove down with a van for us! Again, how God often works in strange, mysterious and very unexpected ways!

Another time my husband said that he thought we should cancel our term life insurance. After all, he was in good health and it was extra money we could use to pay bills. I didn't know why at the time, but I felt very uneasy about that decision and I told him I did not think it was a good idea. As hard as it was for us financially at the time, I felt we needed to keep it, so we did.

Despite all this drama in our lives, Greg's training was coming to a closure, so he felt it was time to start applying to missionary organizations. The one organization that we were both very interested in held a month-long training session, which we had to attend as a family to see if we would qualify. Again, we were heading to a mountain retreat center with four small children from 4 years old down to 4 months old! What a wonderful experience that turned out to be. At the end of the month, the evaluators came to us and said they felt that Greg would make a great overseas missionary, but they did not think I would do very well at all. I was shocked and hurt to hear this. "But why?" I thought. They said as they observed me those last several weeks, they thought that I did not have the stamina to make it in very rough situations. Little did they know that I was suffering with intense stomach pain and had four small children for which to care! However, they were still going to accept us as a family once we passed the physical exams. When I saw the doctor, I told him of my stomach pain and he made nothing of it; however, when he examined Greg, he noticed that his prostate was enlarged and needed to be checked out and cleared of any abnormalities before we could continue the process. He said it was very common in men and nothing to be worried about.

Just before we went for this final physical exam, while taking a walk alone, Greg was conversing with the Lord about our future. The Lord said that He was going to ask something of Greg but to "not be afraid." The Lord assured him that He was not going to take his life. He was simply asking him to "trust Him." Again, I became scared. For what, was the Lord now asking Greg to trust

Him? The Lord did NOT say. He simply asked for his childlike trust. My mind went back to the day I heard Him speak to my heart at puzzle slide. All belongs to God -- my family, our dreams, our very lives. Nothing is ours. I was reminded of Job 1:21 that says: "The Lord gave, and the Lord has taken away. Blessed be the name of the Lord!" Soon I forgot about this talk that the Lord had with Greg and what He was asking of him. He was asking for Greg's trust, but we still wondered why? Little did we know what was about to happen when we got home. I was also reminded of Job 13:15 which says: "Though He test me or slay me, yet will I trust in Him" no matter the circumstances or consequences.

It was now about a week before Christmas and Greg went to a urologist to be checked out. He recommended that a biopsy be taken, yet we wondered why. That sounded more serious than what the doctor at the missionary organization had told us. He made it sound like it was more of a routine check-up. We went to the hospital for what Greg called a very painful procedure. A few days later the doctor called us up personally and said he needed to see us ASAP. Now we were both very scared. What did he find? Was Greg dying? Why were there no symptoms? So many questions. His office was in an old 1800's mansion downtown. Anxiously, we waited for him to call us into his office. As he sat across a huge cherry desk, he leaned forward, and with a smirk on his face, said to my husband sarcastically, "Say good bye to your manhood!" We both were speechless. What was he talking about. It didn't matter. That remark was so uncalled for, I thought no way would he treat my husband with such disrespect, no matter how bad his condition was! He told Greg that he had prostate cancer and that he would need surgery to remove the prostate and to do it as soon as possible. We left the doctor's in total shock and told him that we would get back to him.

Finally, Greg courageously called him and said that he would not undergo the surgery. The doctor, however, put the fear of God into him about his decision. We decided, therefore, to get a second opinion and we went to Johns Hopkins University Hospital. The doctor there was wonderful. He had a terrific bedside manner and was very compassionate. Unfortunately, when we learned of the cost of the surgery, we could not afford to go there. So that door closed. That was one of the most painful Christmas's of our lives. A sick feeling came over both my husband and me. Did we make a mistake thinking we heard from God about being missionaries? Why did he spend all that money on flying lessons? Then, we also found out that Greg was too old to fly with the Missionary organization that we had applied. Our dreams were shattered, and we didn't know which way to turn. When Greg's boss found out that we were no longer able to go to the mission field, he did not want Greg working for him anymore. The only reason he hired Greg was to help him get his mechanics license.

Was my husband going to die and leave me with four small children -- all under the age of four -- to raise by myself? Over the next several months, we had some serious soul searching to do with the Lord. Could we trust Him with our lives and our futures when there did not seem to be a future? No job, no dream, and soon no home. All within a very short time our whole life seemed to fall apart. Hopelessness and despair tried to take over our lives, but we knew that God loved us and had a plan even though we had no idea what that plan was.

He Was There All the Time

What Next, Lord?

Someone told us about a pastor who had cancer and healed himself through a vegetarian diet and drinking lots of carrot juice every day. We got hold of his book and read it desperately hoping it could help us. We started to follow his diet and then decided to go visit him. He had a thriving ministry. Perhaps he would be interested in hiring Greg. We took a family trip to his ministry only to find out he did not have any openings. During this time, we stayed with friends who lived next door to the farmhouse Greg had worked on when I first met him. They were very gracious to house six of us for several months. But that needed to change because we were wearing out our welcome and we did not want our friendship to be ruined because we did not know where to go. We had rented out our farmhouse and the contract was coming to an end. We had told our renters that we would be raising the rent at the end of their contract. They already knew what it was going to be and informed us that they could not afford the increase, so

He Was There All the Time

they moved out and we were able to move in. It was wonderful to have our own place and not feel like gypsies.

Our farmhouse was near a small town and when my husband tried to find a job, nothing came about because he was over qualified. He had been a Wall Street executive, engineer and successful businessman in New York City before we left our jobs to go to bible school. Those "over" qualifications put him out of the job market, especially in our low-income area. He went for interviews and he always did well but when it came time to hire him, he was told that there were no jobs available. We also knew that he was too old and that many companies did not want to pay the kind of salary Greg was used to having. He even told potential employers he would work for much less just to have a job! But still nothing came through for him.

It was Sunday night and Greg took the kids to church for evening service and I told him I wanted to stay home because of severe stomach pain. I was getting depressed because nothing was coming together for him. I decided to look in the paper for a job for him because our bills had to be paid. I prayed and asked the Lord to please give us a miracle because we didn't know where else to turn. When I turned to the employment section, there was nothing for Greg but unexpectedly, a job possibility for me! A school for emotionally disturbed children was looking for a reading specialist so I reluctantly called the school the next morning.

A few days later, I had an interview with the principal and, as I sat there, I had to hold back my tears because I did not want the job. I felt like I was being forced to work because of our situation. I loved being a full-time, stay-at-home Mom and my husband really wanted to work. But unfortunately, the bills were coming in and one of us had to work. In a moment of vulnerability, I started sharing with this principal our desperate family situation. I told her I really did not want to work and my husband, who wanted to work, could not find a job! I also told her about his illness and our having adopted a special needs child. I did have experience working with my child, although I never taught disabled children in school. I also told her what salary we needed to make ends meet. This was a sure interview for disaster, but I could not keep my pent-up emotions in anymore. I just wanted to cry and cry because our family was falling apart. To my surprise, this wonderful lady said we cannot give you the salary you need but I want to hire you!!! Out of desperation, I took the job; however, my health could not keep up with the demands of the job and our family situation at home. I worked with emotionally disturbed, disabled kids all day and then went home to my own child who displayed similar behaviors. It was too much stress on my mind and body.

I tried hard to hold it together, but it was not working. My stomach pain got worse and worse to the point I could barely function. I do not handle physical pain very well. The emotional stress was very difficult to handle too, and as it increased, it acerbated the physical pain. It became a vicious cycle. I could hardly eat and if I did, I could barely keep anything down. This combination of emotional stress and physical pain brought me into severe clinical depression. Greg had to find a job!

We both prayed hard and looked in the paper again. There it was: a nation-wide trucking company was looking for long distance drivers. Hesitantly, Greg went for the interview, knowing his health was not good either. But the interviewer never asked about the cancer and he was hired. He then went into training and learned that once the job officially began, he would be gone for a week or two at a time. This went on for a few months, but I could not handle the children all alone, especially my disabled daughter with her many needs. One day I had a total breakdown and I could not get out of bed. I could not function due to the severe physical and emotional pain of caring for our family and wondering what was going to happen to us if Greg's condition worsened. Although he did not have surgery for the prostate cancer, he did have a radium seed implant. We hoped that the implant would take care of the cancerous cells. Greg believed he was healed and did not want to return to the doctor to be retested to ensure that he was still doing OK. Always in the back of my mind, however, was the fear that it was not all taken care of and that it was still in his body. He would tell me that I lacked faith, so I would let it go and I kept praying instead.

Just before I had my total collapse, I went to a gastroenterologist who finally diagnosed my condition after many years of intense suffering, as Irritable Bowel Syndrome (IBS). It was not a disease, but a malfunction of the colon brought on by emotional stress and eating foods that my body could not digest. When he heard my story and the stress I was under, he said that I needed to see a psychiatrist about my problems. I was terrified to hear this news. Was I going crazy or what? I never expected to hear this from my gastroenterologist. I just thought he would give me some medicine and I would go on with my life. But this was much more serious than I thought.

While he was in the next room calling various doctors to see who would see me, I was in his exam room crying out to God to please send the right doctor who could really help me. Finally, after what seemed a very long time, he came back and said he contacted a doctor who would work with me. When I left his office, I just cried and cried wondering how I would ever break this news to my husband. I decided to stop someplace to call him on the phone so that I could break this news to him gently. I really was scared to pressure him with more problems. The poor man had enough to deal with and now this too!

He Was There All the Time

When I went to the psychiatrist, he gently told me that I had lots of layers that had to be peeled off to get to the root of my problems. He compared it to the peeling of an onion. He asked what my biggest stress was at the time and I told him caring for my husband, who had cancer, and my special needs daughter, who had many needs brought on by being born with fetal alcohol syndrome. Plus, I had three other children who needed the love and care of a mom as well. At the time, the children were all under the age of 8 and they needed a healthy mom and dad yet we both were battling serious health issues. We did the best we could to hold our family together with the help of the Lord but at times I felt hopeless and despairing that things were not going to improve. I really questioned where God was in all of this. My faith was being tested and I felt like it was really being shattered. My disabled daughter's needs were way beyond my ability. I could no longer care for Greg or my other children as well as myself! Therefore, my body took all the pain upon itself until it would not function anymore. I could barely eat so I was losing weight and getting very weak and depressed. Unbeknownst to me at the time, some Christian friends were saying to my husband that he should leave me because of what I was going through. They questioned if I was really a Christian. Thank God, he did not tell me this until many years later when I had gotten well. It took a long time and a lot of prayer for me to forgive them, but I did, knowing that they had no idea what I was experiencing. My husband told them that he would never leave or forsake me. He took our wedding vows very seriously. We would stay together in sickness and in health, until death separated us.

What ultimately led to my emotional breakdown was the recommendation by my psychiatrist to temporarily place our little girl in foster care, so that I could care for Greg and my other three children and get myself well again. That broke my heart and I felt like a total failure as a mom and a Christian. I rationalized that I was the failure and not God because He never gives us more than we can handle. Not only did I fail my family, but I felt I had failed God too! I could not even care for myself let alone the rest of my family. How could this have happened? Did we make mistakes in all our decisions that we had made along the way? I knew that God gives us the strength we need for every situation as we call upon Him each day. We were calling upon Him; however, I was falling apart, and my daughter was being placed in foster care because I could not care for her!

My thinking went from bad to worse to the point that everything I thought was totally negative, hopeless and despairing. Was God even there for us? Did He love us? Would we ever see the light of day again? In a moment of total hopelessness and despair, I am ashamed to say that I did overdose on some pills but was immediately taken to the hospital and cleaned out. I truly understand what it is to live with severe, chronic, debilitating pain and to suffer major depression and to see no way out. BUT GOD saw our situation and he was there not to judge or condemn but to help us in a most unexpected way.

At first, our daughter stayed with several concerned friends. But this did not work out either. Every family that she stayed with experienced similar problems with her out of control behaviors and one by one they would come back to us and say they could not care for her. This only intensified my emotional pain which led to deeper and deeper depression. Who then could help her, if anyone? It finally got to the point that we had to turn to foster care. It broke our hearts, but we had nowhere else to turn. Perhaps my doctor was right. We started the process and once again, she went from family to family until she was placed with a family that could "somewhat care" for her. Unfortunately, to accomplish this, our daughter had to be placed on different drugs that actually caused mild seizures just to control her behavior! Again, my heart broke and I blamed myself for her problems. When she lived with us we just put up with her out of control behaviors without drugs. Now she was being heavily drugged just to get her to function somewhat decently. More guilt, more blame and more depression until one day I literally could not get out of bed.

My husband had to quit his over-the-road trucking job just to be home with me and to help care for the other children. A friend of ours worked as a manager for a fine department store in the furniture department. He saw our desperate situation and offered Greg a job for commission only. Greg was an engineer and not very outgoing. He was very quiet, reserved and not at all pushy like many other sales people. There was no way that we could live on a salary based on commissions. But we had no other choice. After much prayer, Greg decided to trust God with his lack of skills in this area and go work for this man. On the weeks that he sold practically nothing the store would lend him $200.00 that he would have to make up in the next week before his commissions kicked in again. It was a very stressful time for us, but we would pray together that God would bring in the sales and do for Greg what he could not do naturally for himself! And that is exactly what happened. He became a wonderful, humble salesman that people loved. God blessed us in amazing ways and we gave all glory to God for this miracle. Somehow the money we needed always came in and our bills were paid just in time. We never went into debt. During these hard times, my husband said that we would continue to tithe to the Lord first and pay our bills with the remainder of his meager paycheck. As we were faithful to God, He was more than faithful to us.

When I had my total collapse, I was in my early 40's. Daily, I had to ask God for help just to do simple things, like get out of bed, go to the bathroom and wash my face. I hardly had the strength to do these simple tasks. One day as I lay in bed, I heard the Lord speak clearly to my heart: "Just put one foot in front of the other, do first things first and then ask Me what is next on the agenda." For several months, this is how I lived. I would ask the Lord for help just to get out of bed. Then I would ask Him what do I do next? He would say go to the bathroom and wash your face, next brush your teeth and next shower. Many days I was too weak to even shower and I would ask Him for strength just to get into the shower, wash up and wash and dry my hair. He was so faithful and as days and months went by, my strength started to return. I did have some hospitalizations during this period because of the severe depression which was diagnosed as clinical depression. My depression was due to faulty thinking about my stressful life and thyroid issues as well. Eventually the thyroid issue improved, but I still had to work on my thinking and how to respond in healthier ways to my family situation. At one point, my doctor thought that I might never be normal again and told my husband that I might have to be institutionalized because of the severity of my condition. When I heard this, I cried out to God asking Him to advocate for me to really get better. I also asked Him to help me change my thinking. I was desperate. I wanted to be normal again, whatever that was.

Little by little I started the uphill battle against the internal demons of despair, hopelessness, fear and anxiety brought on by my reaction to our family situation. I had to face the fact that our dreams were shattered and that I could not heal, fix or change my special needs daughter, my husband or our family situation. I could not keep my husband alive and cure his cancer either. I also had to accept the fact that I too had a very sensitive stomach that over reacted to stress and all kinds of foods that I really enjoyed. It meant changing my eating habits and lessening my stress levels and trusting God with His will and plans for our lives and not my dreams, will and plans. Bottom line, I had to daily let go of control --control of my life, my husband and children's lives and our future. I had to learn to trust like a child and leave our future in God's hands. This was a very tall order but, if I wanted to get well, I had to just simply let go and learn to live one day at a time and oftentimes one minute at a time.

One sunny winter afternoon, some friends invited us out to their farm, but I was not feeling well so I told my husband to just leave me home and he and the kids go have fun. But he refused to leave me. I insisted that he go but he overrode my persistence and stayed home anyways. That truly was a God inspired decision because later that day, while folding clothes in our upstairs bedroom, he asked me if I smelled smoke. I told him I did not. But he thought it might be coming from our wood burning stove. When he went down to our living room which was just below our bedroom he felt the wall and, sure enough, it was very warm. He then checked the stove and pipe, as well. Next thing smoke and flames

He Was There All the Time

burst out of the wall and our house was on fire! He screamed to all of us to get out of the house immediately. It was a cold wintery day with snow covering the ground, but we got the kids and animals out just in time. The fire department quickly put out the fire before it destroyed our whole house. After this incident was over, I thought to myself this truly was a divine appointment orchestrated by God who really did love us and was looking out for our family. Had Greg gone to our friend's home with the kids, I probably would have died in the fire because I was planning to sleep the whole time they were away. I never smelled any smoke and if it had not been for my husband's sense of smell and fast reaction time, we could all have been killed that day.

One Sunday morning, as we were getting ready to leave for church, our phone rang as we were walking out of the house. Greg asked me if he should answer it or just let it go. We did not want to be late for morning service, but I encouraged him to just answer it quickly to see who it was. To our surprise it was a long-time friend of ours from bible school. He told Greg that he had been trying to find out what happened to us since we all left the school. In a few minutes of time, Greg tried to tell him all that had happened to our family over the last several years. Then he went on to tell Greg that the Lord put our family on his heart and that he had to find us to share some good news with us. He and his family were living in this Christian community in rural Missouri and working with emotionally disturbed children. Perhaps this would be a good place for us to bring our daughter. It all sounded very good, but we didn't have an extra penny to check out this ministry. Every dollar Greg made went to pay our bills, after we tithed, so he told his friend we would pray about it. Greg and I sat down and decided that if we wanted to take a week-long trip out to Missouri from New York, where our farm was, we would need $600.00. Our friend said once we got out there we could stay with his family at their house. But we still needed money for gas, food and hotels.

We had a beautiful prayer cabin on our 110 acres property and I used to love to go out there to be alone with the Lord to pray, listen to His small voice and journal. This was all part of my healing. Learning how to listen to the Lord and seeking His will in all things was now becoming more and more my heart's desire. It was the Monday after the phone call and I went out to our prayer cabin while Greg was at work and the kids were at school. I prayed to the Lord and said, "Lord, if this is your will that out of this very unexpected and mysterious phone call, we go to Missouri to check out this ministry, you will have to provide the money. If you send it then we will know that this, is in fact, your will and not ours. Thy will be done." I let go. I released it and I waited. Within the next few days amazing things happened. I received a letter in the mail from my dad who said that the Lord had put on his heart that he was to send us $400.00 that he had allocated to one of the ministries he supports. The Lord told him to send it to us instead and he did not know why! But he obeyed. Then about two days later, we received a reimbursement check from the insurance company for my daughter's braces. I totally forgot that we paid upfront for her braces and then the insurance company would reimburse us quarterly for their part. The check was for about $174.00. We were $26.00 short of the $600.00 we needed. But we were both in awe at these two very unexpected surprises in answer to our prayers! Another amazing thing happened also. Greg was coming up for vacation time and he had to take it at a certain time and his friend's call came just before he was to take time off from work. Again, the timing was so perfect we could not help but see God's hand in all of this.

We set out for Missouri with our $574.00 and met with the pastor of this wonderful ministry, there in the middle of the country. We told him our pitiful story and he said that this ministry was just right for us. He was sure he could help us with our daughter, but he wanted us to make sure it was God and not him or us calling us to this ministry. He encouraged us to pray and seek God's will. Greg and I both went off separately and prayed, seeking God's will and we both came up with the same answer. Go forward. Green light. We loved being there and did not want to leave but we needed to go back home and keep praying to be sure we had heard from God before making such a drastic move. The pastor said that we would need to have our daughter live with us again but that supports would be in place to help us care for her. On the morning that we were leaving to go back home, we saw the pastor standing on the corner of our friend's street and we wondered why was he out there at 6:00 AM. We stopped to thank him for our wonderful visit and assured him that we would be in touch with our final decision. Then he took Greg's hand and said, "The Lord told me to give this to you." That explained why he was standing on the corner. When we pulled away, Greg opened his hand to find a $100.00 bill! That was way more than the $26.00 we were lacking when we left a week earlier. We had plenty of money to get back home and a lot to think and pray about.

He Was There All the Time

Walking by Faith

While living on our farm, we learned to walk by faith because we never knew how much money Greg would bring home each week. We had to learn to trust God completely for all our needs and not ourselves. Before we had moved to our farm, we had plenty of savings to live on, so it was easy to say we trust in the Lord because we knew we had money in the bank in which to fall back. However, when the money ran out, we had no other place to turn but to the Lord who proved Himself to be a wonderful Father and provider as well.

One day, while visiting with my psychiatrist, we heard a loud crash outside of his office. His office was on a very busy street. Immediately, I had a word from the Lord that someone had crashed into our van! It was parked on the street near his office, so we quickly ran outside to see what happened. Sure enough, it was our van! Someone was driving too fast, lost control and hit it.

He Was There All the Time

I told my doctor that we were in dire need of a new van, but we did not have the money to buy another one. I also told him it wasn't worth very much as a trade-in. However, the Lord told me to trust Him and that He permitted this to happen for a greater good. Sure enough, when the insurance company looked at our vehicle, it gave us more than enough money to get a "new" used van!

Another time, we had a financial need again, and God had a wonderful plan as to how to meet that need. We had a beautiful old barn on our property that was built in the 1800s – but it was falling apart and needed to be torn down. The fire department was willing to burn it down for us, but we were not ready to let it go. BUT GOD had a different plan. One afternoon I took my kids to the shoe store to buy them shoes for school. The store was about 15 minutes from our farmhouse. By the time we got to the store, the sky had turned dark and a sudden storm was upon us. We stayed in the store until we felt safe to drive home again. When we arrived home, I thought I saw a mirage. I asked the kids: "Did we not have a barn when we left for the store? It is not there now! Where is our barn?" When I went into the house, my husband said that a sudden severe, tornado-like wind had just passed through and completely knocked over our barn! I urged him to contact the insurance company and tell them what happened. He said that the barn was so old and that it probably was not covered by our insurance. But I persisted that he make the call just to be absolutely sure. He reluctantly called the insurance company just to appease me! An adjuster was sent out to investigate the situation. Shortly thereafter, word came back that the barn was insured and a check for $16,000.00 was sent to us! Once again, we were in awe as to how the Lord was caring for our family!

I recall another incident. It was October and a dear friend of mine told me that she had gotten a substantial amount of money and wanted to bless our family that Christmas. She insisted that I go shopping and buy whatever my heart desired for my kids. They had the best Christmas opening all these wonderful gifts that Greg and I could never afford to buy. I was forever grateful to her and to God for her very generous heart.

Another Christmas, we had gone to Christmas eve service at our church and when we got home there were two huge black trash bags sitting on our kitchen floor. Puzzled, we opened the bags to find lots of wrapped gifts for our whole family. Only our friends next door had a key to our locked house. We questioned them, and they said they knew nothing about this. We never did find out who blessed us that year or how they got into our home while we were praising the Lord at church.

On still another Christmas, we received a call that our names were chosen to come to a food pantry to select food and gifts for our family. We felt that there were people in greater need than us but, for whatever reason, we were deeply humbled to be the recipients that year. It is truly more blessed to give than to receive but sometimes we must remain humble enough to let others bless us in our times of need.

Another time we were blessed again in a very unexpected way. I had a good friend whose husband was diagnosed with brain cancer. His cancer was far more aggressive than Greg's and we used to pray together in a small prayer group for one other. One day as I was driving down one of our remote country roads, I hit a deer! I was very upset because I knew we had to pay a $500.00 deductible before the insurance would repair our van. I brought this concern up at our prayer meeting, but I never expected God to answer our prayer request in the way He did! My friend came over to our house with a check for $500.00! I felt awful taking this money from her, knowing that her husband was dying! She told me that she and her husband had prayed about it and felt the Lord had blessed them financially and they wanted to pass the blessing onto us! She told me that the Lord put it on her heart to do this for us! Once again, we felt so humbled by this very act of self-less love. Soon after, her young husband did go home to be with the Lord, leaving her to raise three small children alone.

After much prayer, the time came for us to decide if we should leave our beautiful farm, which was like a retreat center for us. We had gone through a lot of pain and suffering due to Greg's cancer, my health issues and our daughter's many problems. While living on our farm, Greg started seeing a urologist at my persistence! Even though he felt I was doubting his healing, I still wanted to "be sure" he was totally healed. Upon the doctor's request, he had another PSA test done and this time it showed that the cancer was very much alive and getting worse than it had previously been! The urologist thought he might be eligible for an experimental drug that was being tested on men with prostate cancer. He sent Greg to Memorial Sloan Kettering Cancer Center in New York City to see if he fit the tight criteria for this experimental drug. It meant taking time off from work and driving several hours or taking a bus into the city every couple of months. He had to agree to all the requirements if he was accepted into the program. So together, we went to Sloan Kettering where a plethora of tests were done to see if he was eligible. The results came back that he was eligible for the new drug. When he started taking the drug, he would get quite sick and weak, but the cancer was regressing! It was during this time, that we received the call from our friend to move out to Missouri to join the ministry that worked with disturbed children. If we did move, Greg would have to continue his treatments and follow ups which he committed to when starting the program. This was a very serious situation which had to be taken into consideration before we decided to uproot our family and make the big move.

He Was There All the Time

It was a sunny, warm spring day as I sat in our gazebo thinking about and meditating on God's will for our lives. As I was praying, I felt the Lord again speak to my heart. As much as I loved our peaceful farm, we had an opportunity to move into a ministry that was willing to take us with all our brokenness and help us be a complete family again. We were also being given the opportunity to help serve others, in similar situations as our own. We did not go looking for this ministry. It came to us waiting for our response. I saw the end of my life flash before me and I had to think about it seriously. Instead of thinking about our comfortable life style, I began to think of our life in the light of eternity. One day, I would stand before God and give an account for what I did for Him. In the light of eternity, which was the better choice? To stay in our comfortable, beautiful, peace-filled home or reach out to others who were hurting and in need. It was a big decision. I said to the Lord that I don't want to get to the end of our lives and see what we could have done for Him and others, but we chose to stay in our safe home which we loved so much. Greg and I continued to pray, and we came to the same decision. We did not go looking for this open door. It came to us, so we picked up the phone and called the pastor out in Missouri to tell him our decision.

This was in June and if we were to make the big move we wanted to do it before school began which in the Midwest was late August. We prayed hard that God would send us the right renters who would appreciate our beautiful home and treat it the way we did. We had beautiful flower and vegetable gardens and lots of land to mow. We had a lovely prayer cabin, a pond and gazebo on our property and flowers around them. We wanted a family who would love and cherish our peaceful "retreat haven" as we did. We hoped that God would send us a Christian family -- or at least a very good family. Our prayers were more than answered. A couple with their son came out to see our home and fell in love with it. They wanted to "try country living before buying a home outside of town." They were wonderful renters who took very good care of our home and grounds and after a short while came to us wanting to buy our home at any price we asked. They had the cash and all we had to do was agree to a good price. However, my husband was not ready to sell our beautiful home. They were saddened but continued to rent from us.

Fast forward: After a few years, my husband said to me one day that he was ready to let go of our farm; however, being very sick, he asked me to call our renters. I was very saddened to hear their news. They had taken the money that they had planned to spend buying our home and bought an auto dealership instead. They no longer had the resources to buy our home. I felt like we missed a blessing, but I knew God must have other plans.

Before we left for Missouri, we sold Greg's sister several acres of our property located atop a hill; however, the only way she could

He Was There All the Time

access her home on the hill was through our driveway. Our renters got to know my sister-in-law and they did not mind that she used the same driveway, but new, prospective buyers did not like the idea of sharing a driveway with someone else. Many people loved our property and home until they learned of this situation and then backed out. It took a very long time before a buyer finally came through and it was not our first choice. In fact, we had to take a huge cut in what the home and property were worth all because of this situation. But we were desperate, so we closed on the deal. Unfortunately, we heard from neighbors that the new owners destroyed our beautiful home and property. It was no longer a peaceful retreat center. It had now become a fallen down dump. My husband and I both grieved this loss, but we realized it's just an earthly home and we were on our way to our heavenly home which was far more beautiful. In the light of eternity, as painful as it was, it was a small trial.

The Move to Missouri

As we set out for Missouri, we felt hope rise in our hearts for the first time in years. This was going to be a new beginning for our family who would be intact again because our daughter would now be back home with us.

The ministry was growing very quickly, and houses were popping up everywhere to care for the many families that were joining it. Just as we were getting ready to leave for Missouri, we received a phone call that a brand-new, state-of-the art home was under construction and that the pastor wanted us to have it. It was huge, with 4 bedrooms and double the size of our farm house. God once again blessed us beyond our wildest dreams. Our pastor blessed both Greg and I with good jobs and very good salaries. I received a wonderful blessing in that I would be able to use my skills as a reading specialist to help children who had severe reading problems. Greg took on various jobs before they found the right one for him. With a strong engineering background, they asked him to be the High School Math and Science teacher. He loved the kids and they loved and respected him. Although he had never taught school before, he became an excellent teacher.

When we moved to Missouri, I made the decision to throw away my anti-depressant drugs and trust in the Lord instead, for my physical health and mental and emotional well-being. I would never recommend this to someone else, but I knew my physical and emotional problems were due to negative, faulty thinking. I did start to feel better, so it turned out to be the right decision; however, on occasion, I did have bouts of IBS attacks when under intense stress. With the Lord's help, I tried to face those issues head on. I still had to watch what I ate, and I also had to watch my thought life to keep my thoughts in check from getting anxious, fearful or worried. I kept turning to the Lord and asking Him how to respond calmly to situations, rather than react impulsively. I realized this was my "thorn in the flesh" that was going to keep me running to the Lord daily to maintain peace of heart, mind and body. To this day, it is a daily surrender to the Lord's will and ways and not mine. It has not been easy, but it keeps me on my knees running to Jesus and MaMa Mary for help and strength especially when I fall back into my old thinking patterns which have an adverse effect on my emotions, which in turn effects my stomach. It is amazing how integrated our body, soul and spirit are! When one part of us is out of whack, it affects the other parts of us as well. We truly are fearfully and wonderfully made.

Unfortunately, the first few months in Missouri were not as we had hoped for our little girl. She had a very hard time adjusting to her new school and surroundings and she refused to listen to her teachers or anyone in authority. She continually acted out in inappropriate ways and was continually being disciplined. Nothing seemed to be working as our pastor thought it would. One day, our friends who had invited us to come out to the ministry said that their daughter, who had now graduated from high school, was willing to work with her one-on-one if the pastor agreed to it. Our pastor thought that this was our last resort, and if this did not work, our daughter would have to go back to public school. As providence would have it, it turned out to be the ideal answer for her. This young woman bonded with our daughter and helped her stay focused while in school.

Then the inevitable came. After a few months, her parents told us that they were leaving the ministry to pursue other plans. We were shattered because their daughter also was leaving. What would happen to our little girl? She was in a special education classroom with a very good special education teacher, but she needed the one on one help to stay calm and get her work done. Unfortunately, this was no longer the case. Our Pastor had a change of heart, however, and decided that our daughter should stay at the Christian school. Between the Special Education teacher and the two classroom aides, our daughter's needs were met in the best way possible.

Greg continued to travel to New York City for his cancer treatments and follow up appointments at Sloan Kettering. We had been in ministry in Missouri about two years when some strange events took place in a matter of a few months. It was January and we once again needed a newer van. We went down to the local dealer and I saw a beautiful one with all kinds of gadgets and gismos. It was beyond our price range, but I thought we could "swing it". As we were talking to the salesman, I said something that made him think that we wanted to buy it. He then said that he would be right back. While he was out of the room, Greg said: "You do realize he thinks we just bought this van." I argued and said, "No that is not true." But a few minutes later the salesman came back with the contract. I felt sick to my stomach! Greg was right! I opened my big mouth and said something that gave the salesman the impression it was a done deal. Greg was quite upset with me but so was I upset with myself. I apologized to Greg profusely. I'm sure we could have backed out of the deal, but Greg saw how much I loved this van! Little did we know at the time that this was part of a bigger plan than we realized. God was up to something that we were not yet privy to.

After this incident, two other very strange things happened. A good friend of ours asked if we had ever seen the movie *Inn of the Sixth Happiness.* I told her that no, we had never heard about or seen it. She then said she knew how we all wanted to be overseas missionaries. This movie was about a woman who became a missionary in China. Of course, we wanted to see it, even if we could never go there ourselves. She loaned it to us and that sparked a flame that had long died when we found out that Greg had cancer. However, it also left us feeling very sad inside because we knew this dream would never be actualized in our lives. BUT GOD had other reasons for her loaning us that film. Little did she know at the time that the Lord was using her to prepare us for something very special! The timing of it was incredible.

Shortly thereafter, another very strange thing happened to me, this time in one of my classes. One of my students, a young teen age girl, told me that she had a gift for me. None of my students ever brought me gifts because most of them were living in our ministry's group home and they had little or no money. She had been shopping with her mother who came to visit her that previous weekend. While in a variety store, she saw this beautifully wrapped bar of soap that had come from China. The wrapping was all torn but the writing on it was in Chinese. She told me that when she saw it, it reminded her of me. She asked her mother if she could buy it for me and her mother readily agreed. She then apologized about the wrapping being torn. I graciously accepted her gift and wondered why in the world a student would buy me a bar of Chinese soap? Was this another God incident? Only time would tell.

March was always a very hard month for us emotionally because we would have a missionary conference at our church for several days. Missionaries from all over the world would come and speak to us and this left Greg and I feeling very sad inside. We loved hearing their wonderful stories, but we knew that we could never experience mission life for ourselves. We had reconciled ourselves that our ministry in the heartland is what God had in mind for us. We loved what we were doing but we felt called in another place that just didn't seem to be working out for us. BUT GOD had different plans once again! Why did we feel so torn inside? Our children were all doing very well. They were involved in sports and band and life seemed to be going along quite well. Even our special needs daughter was settling down and adjusting as best as she could. So why the ache in our hearts?

Then something very strange happened one night. After the evening conference was over, while Greg was talking with someone, I slipped away to talk with one of the missionaries from South America. He was telling me of all the wonderful things happening in his ministry, and as he was talking, I had another one of those strange encounters with the Lord. I heard His voice speak loud and clear to my heart. "Get ready! I am going to send you to the mission field." I couldn't believe what I was hearing. But once again I argued with the still small voice and said, "But Lord, what about Greg's cancer?" And the voice said: "It will no longer be an issue." It all happened so quickly, and I immediately went back to listening to this missionary tell me about his work. I then said to myself: "But where, Lord are you going to send us?" I did not get an answer. When Greg finally found me, I told him what had just happened, and he said let's just keep on praying and wait on the Lord to see what He shows us. My husband was a very prayerful, wise man. He never wanted to do things in his strength or his timing. If it was from the Lord, he felt it would come to pass. Being human, we did not always walk in the ways and timing of the Lord, but in His great mercy, the Lord always had a way of getting us back on track.

About two weeks later, our pastor did something he had never done before. He brought in a missionary from a mission college to tell our church about some great works the Lord was doing throughout the world, particularly in China. We learned that the harvest was plentiful but the laborers few. This missionary then held a separate meeting for those who were seriously interested in learning more about this great work of evangelism in China. At first, I was not at all interested in attending this special meeting

He Was There All the Time

because I could not handle more heart pain knowing we could not be a part of this great move of God. Greg, on the other hand was very interested in hearing what this missionary had to say so he informed me that with or without me, he was going. After much prayer, I decided to join him. After all, the Lord did speak that special word to me, two weeks prior to this unusual event. Could this possibly be what the Lord was preparing us for??? The missionary shared that the people in China were hungry for God and there was a great need for missionaries to share the gospel with the Chinese people. He then said if any of us were serious about being overseas missionaries, come see him after the lecture. My heart started pounding and I thought the whole room could hear it. I was ready to explode inside, and I tapped my husband and he said to just listen. Afterwards, I asked him what he thought, and he said he had the same feelings also. We went up to the man and asked for information about this ministry that he represented. He told us what website to go to start the application process. By faith, we started the process.

The timing of this whole event was incredible again. It was now April and Greg was to go back to Sloan Kettering for his follow-up appointment in May. His appointment was the Monday after Mother's Day. At this point, Greg felt we needed to see our pastor and tell him what was happening in our hearts. At first, our pastor was taken aback by our news. Being a very wise and practical man, he said that he had been in China during World War II and not much had improved in their way of life there. He was very concerned for Greg's health. He said that he would need to know that Greg had a clean bill of health before he could send us there with his blessing. He asked when were we thinking of going, and we told him August. Needless to say, he was shocked. He told us that we needed to raise financial support for our family of six and that could take a few years not a few months! We then told him that Greg had an upcoming appointment with his oncologist in May. He encouraged us to keep praying and asking the Lord for His clear will and direction. He promised to pray for us as well. Our pastor was a man of deep prayer and when he said he would pray for you, he really meant it. We had come to love and respect him.

Unbeknownst to the children we were teaching -- including our own -- we never said a word about any of this. But we did tell all the students at school that Greg was going to see his cancer doctor and we needed them to pray that he would be told he had a clean bill of health. That Sunday, as I was walking into church, I heard the Lord speak to my heart again: "This is going to be your happiest Mother's Day ever." I held onto those powerful words as I awaited Greg's call to me the next day. He promised to call and let me know what the doctor had told him. Anxiously I awaited that dreadful moment, but it turned out to be a moment of rejoicing. His

He Was There All the Time

doctor told him that all the previous tests from his last visit showed no cancer at all! He then told her about wanting to go to China as a missionary and she encouraged him to do it! She was a Jewish doctor who showed great kindness to her patients, treating each one as if they were a family member. She supported Greg in his desire to be a missionary; however, she could not say that he was totally healed; instead, she could say that his cancer was in remission. She gave him her blessing as he finished the experimental program, and he never had to go back to her again. As one chapter in our life was closing, another was opening.

When Greg returned home, we went to our pastor to share with him the "good news." He was very happy for us, but he was still very concerned about the timing of when we wanted to leave for China. He asked why the urgency. We told him that we were going to teach English at a university beginning in September and that we needed to be there before classes began. We also told him, due to Communist rule, you just can't be a missionary openly in China -- which he was aware. We had to have an overt job to gain entry into China, and being that we both were teachers, the university opened the door for us to teach there. This unique university was started by a Chinese Christian man who came to America as a child. He wanted to reach young people from his native country with the gospel and what better way than to open a university and send missionaries to teach at his school! God's ways are remarkable!

Our pastor reminded us that our school ended in June which gave us less than two months to raise financial support. We said that if this was God's will, the support would come in. He asked us to put together a budget that would support our family while living in China. We knew we would get a little stipend for teaching but not enough to care for our children's needs. Greg came up with a budget with which our pastor agreed.

During this time, two more very unexpected events occurred. Our friends, who originally had told us about the Missouri ministry, had moved back to their home town. When we went to their home to say our good byes, they said they knew of a lady who was a missionary in China. While we were there, they contacted their friend and discovered that she was on home leave. The timing was amazing, and she agreed to meet with us. We learned so much about China. One of the critical things we needed to know was that the Chinese government – and the Communist Party that controlled it – often placed intelligence operatives posing as students in classrooms to keep track of foreign instructors. Having worked Russian intelligence for years, I felt the Lord had prepared me for such a time as this. I now realized why the Lord led me into the FBI and into the work I did. I really believed that it was to prepare us for this missionary work! Again, I was in awe over all of this and how our lives were truly planned by the Lord from before we were born. From my experience, I knew what to look for in a "spy" and I helped my husband to look for those same signs as well.

Just before we left for China, another friend told us that she knew of a woman who was a nurse/missionary in China and she too was on home leave. Our friend brought us together and this nurse missionary confirmed much of what we already had heard. Now two people had well prepared us for what was to come when we arrived in China. Again, we were amazed at how God had orchestrated all these events.

As Greg and I continued to pray as to how to raise the financial support we needed, we came up with the idea of selling most of the beautiful furniture which we had acquired over the years. When we moved to Missouri, we were making decent incomes, so we bought some beautiful furniture to fill up our very large house. We decided to have a couple of yard sales and they both brought in plenty of income. For our wedding, my mom and dad had given us a lovely, very expensive sterling silverware set. We had never used it because I hated cleaning the silver, so I called dad to find out its value. He told me that, unfortunately, silver had gone down in value and we would get very little for it. But I decided to trust the Lord and place an ad in the local paper for it. I asked for its original value. I soon received a phone call from a woman who said that her daughter was getting married and that she was looking for that very pattern we were trying to sell. She asked if she could come over the next day with cash and we agreed to it. We quickly cleaned up the silver and when she saw how beautiful and new it looked, she bought it for $800.00, the same price my parents had paid for it!

June rolled around quickly, and we were going to have to make a trip out east to visit our families and raise more financial support. We only had about two months in which to do it. We now had a beautiful van that could take us on this lengthy trip. Our pastor agreed to continue to pay us our salaries as well! What an incredible gift. Then came another gift from him. Greg asked our pastor if he would be interested in buying our van after we left for China. He not only agreed to it, but he bought it for the price we paid! In fact, he bought it from us before we set out east! The van now belonged to the ministry, so we did not have to make further payments while raising support. He told us to take the van on our trip and use it until we left for China. We felt so loved. He then said that he wanted to support us while we were in China as well. My parents were very supportive also and between our pastor's support and that of my parents along with many friends, our financial needs were met way beyond what we hoped. God had truly blessed us in ways we never dreamed or imagined all within a few months!

He Was There All the Time

When it was time to leave for China, I packed away that "Chinese bar of soap" that my student had given me because I saw this as God's way of saying "I put it on her heart to give you hope when there was no hope left in your heart."

A New Adventure Begins

This was a very exciting time for our family as we prepared to take this next, huge step in our lives. The flight to China itself was very long and the entire trip took about 30 hours by the time we arrived at the university. We were all exhausted. Our first culture shock was the restroom at the airport in China. There were no toilet seats, just a squatty potty on the floor. This was most upsetting to my girls because they never had been exposed to a potty like this before and they didn't know what to do. Despite their initial reaction, they quickly adjusted!

On the up side, we were greeted by the staff of the school with flowers and warm hugs. They were so happy to see us at that very late hour – almost midnight. By the time we arrived at the school, it was well after midnight and we were exhausted; yet they had a party planned for us. The food looked delicious but all we wanted was to go to bed! We politely told them that our children needed to rest so they took us to our flat which was really two flats side by side with a door separating them. Each flat had one bedroom, a small walk through kitchenette with a sink and counter, a bathroom with a "real western toilet" and a small living room. Greg and I had our own bedroom and we gave the other bedroom in the second flat to the three girls. We converted the second living room into our son's bedroom and my office. Greg worked out of our bedroom. During our two-year stay, we homeschooled our children even though our Chinese hosts wanted them to attend the local schools. We did not want them to fall behind in their American studies, so we opted out of their suggestion.

After we recovered from jet lag, we started the process of unpacking and settling in. We did not have much time as classes were about to begin. While I was unpacking, Greg said that he would go into town to buy some necessary items that we would need such as soap, shampoo, snack foods etc. When he returned, he told me that he had found this unique one-of-a kind store on one of the side streets. He was fascinated by it and decided to buy our necessary items there. When I pulled the items out of the bag, there was that same bar of soap that my student had given me just several months prior to our coming to China! I couldn't believe it. I asked Greg if he realized that it was the same soap that she had given me, and he said no. There were several varieties to choose from, but he randomly chose this one. The only difference was in the color of the wrapping, but the characters were the same. I took this as a sign that we were meant to be here and that the Lord had used my student to prepare us for this mission. What is even more strange is that when we went to other stores to do our shopping, no other store but this one carried this specific soap! I kept this bar of soap on my dresser next to the one my student had given me to remind me that this was truly another act of God letting us know He was with us and He had guided us here using a bar of soap!

While in China, we had a friend back home who would send us bilingual (Chinese-English) bibles packaged in large cereal boxes. Students would come to our flat and ask us to tell them about our God. One of my students came to me one day and said please tell me about your "ghost." We also had other students who were conducting underground services and bible studies and they would secretly come to our flat asking for bibles to take back home to their provinces. It was so exciting to be a part of this wonderful work that God was doing in China. We loved it so much that we wanted to live there forever, die there and be buried there! Again, when I looked back on my life, I saw how God had used many events to prepare us for what He had destined us to do in China. Everything that happened had a future purpose, even though we did not know it at the time.

He Was There All the Time

Our first year in China was fantastic. We saw so many students give their hearts to the Lord and, for the first time in their lives, learn how to pray. They were so spiritually hungry, and it was a wonderful experience to be a part of their new- found faith in Jesus. They would cry as they prayed to Jesus in Chinese and we knew something was happening in their hearts even though we did not speak Chinese ourselves. We were very careful with whom we shared our faith because of the warnings we had received from those two women missionaries that we had talked with before coming to China.

However, we did have some eye-opening experiences, as well, that were not so pleasant. Soon after we arrived in China, our special needs daughter became dehydrated and very sick. She had to be taken to the local hospital by a make shift ambulance which was a beaten-up truck with a board for a bed in it. Someone from the school took us to the hospital and translated for us. Her condition went from bad to worse and the doctors decided they needed to keep her there overnight. When they placed her in a room, they gave me a bed in the same room which turned out to be a board with a very thin cushion. Not at all what we would call a comfortable bed mattress. My daughter was miserable because of these conditions. They put an IV into her and finally she fell asleep. I had a young student – my translator -- share the small twin bed with me. I was at one end and she at the other. Although it was very uncomfortable, she did not seem to mind this at all.

Like the emergency room, the room was disgustingly filthy, but the doctors and nurses were very clean in their white medical garbs. The needles all came out of tightly packaged containers and they too were sterile. I prayed hard to look past the circumstances and at the wonderful care our daughter was receiving from these fine people. There was no bathroom in her room so whenever she had to go, it was my responsibility to help her go in the bed pan. It was also my responsibility to provide food for her. Greg would come by and bring us both meals while we were there. Our daughter was in the hospital for about three days and after that she was totally well -- as if she had never been sick. The doctors gave her a combination of eastern and western medicines and whatever they did worked. She left that hospital a new young woman!

I must share a very funny story. When I needed to use the bathroom, there was a lady's room down the corridor. But it was not like anything I had ever experienced before. There were no private stalls. It was just one long latrine with a short wall separating you from the next person. What made it worse was that there was no door leading into the bathroom, so passers-by could see you going to the bathroom! Men would walk by and look inside which made it a very disconcerting experience to say the least. I

He Was There All the Time

would try to find a section in the corner that was far from the door so that no one could see me squat down to do my business!

When it came time to pay the bill we had no idea what to expect but we were ready to pay whatever the cost just to have our daughter well again. To our shocking surprise it did not amount to very much at all! That made up for the trials we had just been through. Welcome to China, I thought!

One of the things my girls and I loved were the very inexpensive foot and body massages. For less than US $3.00, we could get a wonderful, one-hour massage. These massages became an enjoyable treat that we enjoyed doing together. We also loved biking in the nearby country. We had lots of fun seeing the sights and watching the looks on people's faces as we rode by as a family. We were very unique in this part of China because we were a large foreign family and very few foreigners had been to this part of China. The only foreigners the Chinese had ever seen were on TV.

One day, we went to get our hair cut and one of the beauticians started chasing my son around the room because he had never seen a little boy with light blond hair. He just wanted to touch my son's hair. My son got scared and swiftly ran under a chair and would not come out until this man stopped pursuing him. In fact, this was not the first time this had happened to him. One other time while walking down a street, a lady wanted to pat his head because she had never seen a towhead child like this either. We were warned that this would probably happen to him and sure enough it did!

Greg and I decided that we wanted to stay at a very classy hotel for our wedding anniversary. We hired someone to watch our children while we made our way to this very American looking Holiday Inn. But American it was not. There was a hot tub to which I was looking forward until I went in. The water was freezing. I tried to ask why the water was not hot but no one on the staff understood my question. I gave up my idea of relaxing in a hot tub!

We saw an advertisement in the hotel restaurant that prime rib was the evening specialty. Oh, that was also something I was looking forward to. Perhaps the hot tub did not work out, but a wonderful dinner was still ahead of us. We both ordered the special of the day but were shocked to see what we got! The dinner came on a huge plate -- much bigger than our American dinner plates -- and on it was a huge bone with just a little meat wrapped around it. I tried to explain to the waiter that I wanted prime rib and he told me this was prime rib! Oh my, the rib with hardly any meat. Once again, I had to remind myself that we were in China to die to our flesh and serve the Lord no matter how our flesh felt about it. It was a very disappointing weekend for both of us. We went to this elegant hotel to be refreshed and instead we had more let downs than blessings!

Sundays were special days for us. The school provided transportation to the local Christian church and we always took some students with us who served as our translators. We really wanted them to go so that they could hear the Gospel preached and better understand what we were teaching in bible studies during the week. The students loved coming to church with us and we were blessed to see many conversions.

However, not all of them were sincere. Thank God for my intelligence background because, with God's grace, I detected a student I believed to be a government agent. One day, I received a call from a young man claiming to be one of my former students. He wanted to visit me. I wondered why he wanted to see me when he was no longer my student, but I agreed to a visit. When he came to our flat, the first thing he asked me was a question about another teacher he had. He told me that she told the class that she had worked for the FBI and he wanted to know what I knew about her! She had mentioned something to us at lunch about some work she had done with the FBI, but I never delved into it because I was not allowed to talk about that part of my life while in China. I asked him why he didn't talk to her directly. I acted confused and naïve about the whole situation. I chose to play his game. He then started asking me lots of personal questions which most students never did. By the end of the meeting, he asked if he could get a picture of us together and I told him there was no one home to take it and he quickly retorted that he had a pod to stand the camera on. Most, if not all, of my students were very poor and did not have fancy cameras or pods; nor did they dress to kill like this young man. I could tell he was not like my other students. I knew he was taking my picture for the government to see but they already had my picture, so I was not worried. I just acted like I did not know anything. Then he asked if he could use our bathroom and this was a "no, no" for most Chinese who were so modest. They would never ask to use your bathroom, but this young man was very bold. I got concerned when he was in there quite a long time. I wondered what in the world he really was doing in there. He left the door open a crack, but I could not see what he was doing. I wondered if he was placing a listening device in there to record our conversations. I finally asked if he was OK and he said he would be out shortly. As he was leaving, he asked if I went to church on Sundays and then I knew he was onto something! I told him yes, of course! I even asked if he would like to come with me and quickly he said NO! I knew then that he was an agent who had targeted me because most students couldn't wait to go to church with us.

We did a lot of traveling and saw how people lived in China. They were very poor but very loving. Whenever one of us was sick, they

He Was There All the Time

were right there to accompany us to the doctor to help us get the care we needed. In China, medical care is very different than in America. I recall being very sick, one time and with limited English, my student tried to explain to the doctor my problem. He looked up my "condition" in his little black, medical book and then prescribed an IV full of eastern medicines as well as western antibiotics. I was sent to a small room and asked to lay down on a board while they hooked me up to an IV. I would undergo this treatment for three days. I was so sick that first day, I could hardly walk to the clinic. The IV would last a couple of hours. Then I went back to our flat and drank the Chinese teas he prescribed and took the meds as well. After the third day, I was completely back to my normal self! I was so impressed with this method of helping people to get well. Another time, the doctor wanted me to have a shot in my behind. Well the waiting room and the treatment room were one and the same, so I was told to bend over in front of all these people and pull down my pants while the nurse gave me the shot. A very humbling experience, but once again life in China is very different than here in the USA.

On another occasion, my IBS flared up and I started bleeding very heavily rectally. The doctor said that I had to go for a colonoscopy at the hospital to rule out anything serious such as cancer. The prep was just the same in China as it was back in the US. It was awful, but I complied with doctor's orders. When I arrived at the hospital I was told what was going to happen. I then asked what about the anesthesia? They acted so surprised by my question! I was told that they don't use it in China because it is too expensive. I was so weak and sick I could not undergo any more pain. Right there in the hospital I put my foot down and said: "No! I will not go through with this." I felt like a wimp as I told them, in the United States we always put people asleep when going through this very painful procedure. The school staff – who had arranged the appointment -- became upset with me because they had to schedule another appointment for me at another hospital that would do it with the anesthesia. They also informed me that it was very expensive – by Chinese standards -- but Greg agreed to pay for it.

Once again, I had to go through all the preliminary work up which I hated. For someone with IBS, flushing out one's system is very painful. But I had to do it, not once but twice! When we arrived at the hospital there was a large waiting room with several people waiting to have their procedure done. The doctor was in the next room with the nurse taking one patient at a time. We were like a herd of cattle waiting our turn to get on the table to be tested. And once again there was no privacy! The door stayed open so we all saw the person undress, get on the table and get this procedure done. When the procedure was over, the nurse would quickly shake you up to get you out of sleep and push you out the door.

He Was There All the Time

This was a very humiliating experience, but I had no choice. I felt all eyes were on me because I was the only foreigner in the waiting room. I wondered if most of these people had never seen a foreigner before. This was another death to pride.

But the results were even more humbling than the procedure itself. When I met with the doctor to review my results, he told me -- through a translator -- that there was nothing wrong with me physically and that the problems were all in my head! He then said get your spirit and soul right and your body would be healthy. I was embarrassed to think that here I was a missionary sharing the Gospel and I was having spiritual and emotional problems myself! Once again, I felt like a failure as a Christian. I kept thinking about what this doctor said: change your thinking, change your thinking. I was frustrated because we were having serious problems with our special needs daughter once again and Greg was having problems with his health as well.

After a year and a half of being in China, it became apparent that we had to take our daughter back to the states if we were to finish our two-year contract with the school. But who would care for her while we finished our work there? I tried writing to our pastor in Missouri, but I received no answer. I tried a second time but still no answer. I asked friends at the ministry to pray for us that God would open a door for her to stay somewhere until we finished our two-year commitment. It was a very tall order because people at the ministry knew of our daughter's problems. How could anyone care for her while we were clear across the world? One day as I was walking across the campus I said: "Lord we need to have an answer soon." Christmas was coming and with that, a break from school. I needed to take our daughter back to America but to whom I thought? By faith, we made plane reservations for all of us to go home for Christmas break, not knowing with whom my daughter was going to stay when we got there! Soon after I had prayed this prayer to the Lord, a friend contacted us and said that she would take our daughter if our pastor agreed to it. He was hesitant at first because of our being so far away but he finally agreed that it would only be for 6 months. Once again God heard and answered our prayers prayed in blind faith before we saw the answer!

I don't recall why, but I remember Greg had to stay back in China and fly home about a week later than our children and me. When we arrived at the Beijing Airport, I could not figure out how to do all the paper work and no one was able to help me. When I reached the counter to show the agent our passports, he kept shaking his head that something was wrong with my paperwork. I was getting very nervous because he would not let us get past him to get to our plane. I kept trying to tell him we need to get to our plane and time was getting short, but he spoke no English and neither did anyone else around us. I prayed hard that the Lord would intervene and bring about a miracle to help us. Then, two beautiful Chinese ladies came literally out of nowhere to us in line and pointed to their watch that we need to hurry. I tried to tell them that the customs agent would not allow us to get past him! They didn't understand me, but they took the situation into their hands and decided to talk to him themselves. In a matter of minutes, these two sweet ladies convinced the official to let us through and then grabbed our luggage and hurried us along to our plane which was on the other side of the airport. I would never have found it on our own as they kept turning down different aisles! Finally, we arrived at our gate as the other passengers were in line getting ready to board. We were one of the last ones to board. When I turned to thank these two ladies, they were gone! I do believe that God sent two angels to get us to the plane just in time.

When we arrived in Los Angeles, we could not get to our connecting flight on time. We landed in the international terminal and we had to get to the domestic one. We had to take a bus to get there. Everyone was very tired and irritable, which made our getting from one place to another much slower. While waiting for the bus, a nice gentleman saw my need and helped us with our luggage from the bus stop to the counter inside the terminal. When we arrived at the counter, we were told the gate had closed and we had missed our flight. I told the agent that it was not our fault, but she gave me a hard time. I told her I should not have to buy new tickets for all five of us. Then this man stepped in and fought for us and he got us on another flight at no extra cost to us! After this was over, he asked for some money for helping us out. I gladly gave him $50.00, which was a lot less than purchasing tickets for five of us. Once again, I thought he was a Godsend. God knew we were going to have this trial and He just so happened to have this man standing at the bus terminal waiting to help someone. We found out that this was illegal but that day I was thrilled he got away with it. There were signs all around the airport with respect to loitering, but he did it anyways!

When Greg arrived back in Missouri, something else happened which was very disturbing. One morning, as my husband was leaving the ministry hotel, he fell to the ground. Perhaps he slipped on the ice, we thought, but he was usually very careful, so this puzzled us. He told me what happened, so we thought he needed to see a chiropractor because he was in pain. He went to the chiropractor and they did x-rays but nothing showed up. He later fell again. The pain got worse, so I suggested maybe we should not go back to China. He then said we will finish what we started. We settled our daughter in her new home and then went to the airport only to be met with more difficulties. As Greg bent over to tie his sneakers after going through security, excruciating pain went through his hip and leg and he could barely get up and walk. I said again, perhaps we should stay home but he insisted

He Was There All the Time

that we go back to China. Our departure gate was way at the end of the airport and Greg could no longer carry his bags, so the children and I helped him out. I was very worried about him. Not only did our special needs daughter have major problems that had to be dealt with but now Greg did too! The 30-hour trip back to China was a real test for Greg because of the severe pain he had in his lower back, hip and leg. When we returned to our flat Greg recalled that he had been having lower back problems when he sat at his computer chair. He blamed the pain on the poor quality of the chair, so we got another chair. But the pain only worsened.

Over the next several months Greg's pain got so bad that he could hardly get out of bed to walk across the campus to teach his classes. We would ask other missionaries to come to our room and lay hands on him and pray that he would have the strength to get up and teach. Barely was he able to do it but he did by God's grace! I finally convinced him to go for a full body massage thinking that this might help. However, when he went to the clinic, he was advised by the clinician to go to the hospital instead. Through a translator, he said that Greg needed more care than he could provide. Now I was really getting worried.

Greg went to the hospital and an MRI showed a problem but due to poor translation we were told it was "old man's disease." What was old man's disease we thought? Perhaps it was arthritis. We just didn't know what to think of this prognosis. But the doctor recommended that he come to the hospital a few times a week for therapy for the pain. They did all kinds of strange things to my husband like put a hot glass jar over the areas of pain to pull the pain out. After the procedure was done, he felt much better-pain free! But no sooner than we returned to our flat, it came back again. By the time our contract was fulfilled, Greg had lost a lot of weight, could barely eat or walk, and was very weak. I knew something was terribly wrong. Before we returned to the States, we contacted our doctor back in Missouri who made an appointment for Greg to see a very good doctor of osteopathy.

He Was There All the Time

Home Again in the Heartland

When Greg saw the doctor and told him of all his symptoms, the doctor told him that he thought Greg's prostate cancer had returned and had spread to his bones. Further testing proved this to be the case. We were both in shock to hear this news. Now what? Where do we turn? We had no jobs and no insurance. Greg said that we should check with the Veterans Administration (VA) because he had served in the military when he was young.

Fortunately, the VA accepted him, and Greg saw a doctor concerning treatments for his cancer. He went for one treatment and the side-effects were so nasty that he decided to trust the Lord with his life rather than this medication. The doctor told him that there was no cure but with this medication he would live about 18 months. But there was no quality of life except more excruciating pain due to the side effects. He let the medication go letting God decide how long he would live. He was with us for 28 months. 10

months longer than he would have been had he continued with the treatment.

When we returned to Missouri, we had no place to stay; however, a home just so happened to be vacant and our pastor decided to give it to us. This was Greg's most favorite home at the ministry. He always wished he could live in this lovely corner lot home and now his wish came true without us saying a word. This truly was another God incident.

To our surprise, families came together and filled the cupboards with food and furniture for each of our rooms. We still had to buy some necessities, but the home was ready for us to move in. What a blessing it was to be a part of such a wonderful Christian community. Not only did our pastor take us back and give us a wonderful home, but he also gave us jobs as well. Even though Greg was very sick and unable to work, he gave him a salary and said when he was ready, he could return to the school and teach once again. I too was given back my reading job. With our jobs came the medical insurance which we badly needed because of Greg's health. It was a rough adjustment returning to the United States after spending two wonderful years in China. They were very difficult years because of the problems we endured; however, they were the two best years of our life. As I pondered my life up to that point, I saw how the Lord fulfilled the dreams He had put in my heart as a 12-year old child. All my dreams had been fulfilled in a way I would never have imagined or expected. I was happily married with four beautiful children. God opened the door for us to adopt a child who was born with severe disabilities and we spent two years as missionaries in a wonderful country where we got to be a part of God's plan of salvation for so many young people. We could not have been more blessed. Now the question rose in my heart: was the Lord going to take my husband home to Himself or heal him?

With each passing week Greg fought back the pain by doing little things like getting out of bed and showering. He eventually went back to teaching but with great exhaustion. Even though he was working with troubled youth, they were always obedient and respectful toward him because they saw how much pain he was in. At this point, my principal gave me a job in the office. I had a cot for sick students to use during the day and, instead of sick students using it, my husband would use it in between classes. He would rest to get strength to teach his next class. This went on for months. The students came to love and honor him. They saw a man who was full of the love of the Lord for them and who wanted to do all he could to help them succeed despite his own pain and suffering. I too sat back in awe because I knew how much effort went into his getting out of bed each day just to get to class.

He Was There All the Time

One of Greg's students came from a very poor part of town yet wanted to make something of his life. He told Greg he wanted to go to a very prestigious school and eventually become an attorney; however, he did not do well on his SAT exam. Greg told him he would stay after school and help him learn the facts he needed to retake the test and try again to get into this school. Not only did this young man's scores rise considerably but he was selected to go to this prestigious school.

After a very long fight, however, Greg's body weakened to the point where he could no longer work. He was offered radiation to help combat the pain, but he was too weak to go to the treatment center which was an hour's drive away. I prayed once again that we could find a place to stay while he went through his month-long radiation treatments several times a week. After calling various hotels and bed and breakfasts in this small college town, a wonderful place opened for us to stay. It was a bed and breakfast that had a separate entrance to this apartment. We would not bother the other guests staying in the main house. Daily, I helped Greg get to his appointments. He could barely walk or eat at this point and he slept most of the day. After his treatments, the bed would be soaking wet and we had to change sheets at least once – if not more -- a day. I asked the doctor if this was a side effect of the radiation and he said he never heard of this happening.

One day I nearly lost it. Greg was feeling a little better -- more like his old self -- and he suggested we go out to an ice cream shop for some ice cream. I was so excited to see this spark of life in him, so I gladly complied. But what happened there really upset me. As we left the shop, he started acting like a little boy which was totally out of character for my husband. In fact, his whole personality changed. When we got back to our apartment, he took a broom stick and acted like it was his horse. He totally acted like a little child and I couldn't help wondering if the radiation was messing with his mind as well. After these two incidents, he immediately went back to being real sick and barely able to get out of bed.

My heart also broke for our four children who were still back at the ministry. I knew they were suffering terribly, as well knowing that their father might die soon. Thank God that the wonderful family who took our daughter in decided to keep her when we returned from China. They realized I needed to put my focus on Greg, so they lifted this burden from my heart. Our little girl really wanted to be home with us, but I could not care for her many needs and those of Greg as well. She continued to act out in defiance, but this family dealt with it as best as they could just to help us out.

One day, while staying at the bed and breakfast, I received a call from good friends who would be traveling to Missouri and were willing to drive three hours one way from where they were staying just to see Greg and pray for him. What love I thought! The husband played his guitar and together we worshiped the Lord and had our own little prayer service. It was very special and, although Greg could barely stay awake, he too was blessed by this loving gesture.

Finally, the radiation treatments were over, and we went back home to the ministry. Greg was now so weak he could barely get out of bed and hospice needed to be called. Through it all, Greg kept telling me to keep the faith and not give up on his healing. Those were hard days as I tried to keep the faith while watching his body wither down to nothing! At this point, our pastor called me in and said that he needed to remove Greg from the payroll but that he would keep me on the payroll as a full-time care giver for my husband. I already was doing this in between working, but now I was released to just care lovingly for Greg.

Every morning our pastor would rise about 3:30 AM and go to prayer from 4:00-6:00 AM in our church/gym. Oftentimes, before Greg became real sick, he too would join our pastor in prayer. Occasionally, I would join them also. It was a time of contemplative, silent prayer between our Lord and ourselves. It was very peaceful and quiet as we walked around the gym in darkness except for the red emergency lights shining near the exits. But something now changed. Greg could no longer join our pastor, so he came to Greg and told him that he wanted to come to our home in the morning and pray in our living room instead. We would leave the front door unlocked and a little night lamp on for him. When I would get up during the night, there was our pastor, sitting on a chair in prayer. That touched my heart very deeply. I will always hold this man in high esteem for what he did, not only for Greg but for our whole family. When we saw no future for our family and our dreams shattered, he said to us: "Come join our ministry because we need you and you can be a blessing to many others." He felt because of our trials, we could help others who had gone through severe trials as well. Little did we know how blessed we would be by coming there! In giving, we received more!

When hospice came to our aid in October, I asked how much longer would Greg be with us. They replied that it was only a "guess-timation," but they thought he would be gone by Christmas. Each day was like precious gold to us. We knew his days with us were now numbered. Friends and family came to say their good-byes and Greg asked family members for forgiveness for any hurts he had caused them through the years. I saw lots of tears flowing on both sides as people cried together with him. I saw love being poured out and the hand of God watching over each final encounter. Those were touching moments.

Thanksgiving was quickly approaching, and I had no energy to prepare a Thanksgiving dinner for my family when my husband was dying in the next room. But again, friends came through and made us a beautiful dinner. The Wednesday before, however, something very strange happened. I was praying in our living room and I told the Lord I could not handle this situation any more. I was trying hard to hold on and believe for Greg's healing, but the truth was, he was dying. Greg kept telling me to not give up hope and I tried hard, but I was getting too weak to try anymore. I felt I was quickly losing my grip. I did the very thing I was most afraid to do. I said "OK Lord he is yours. I ask you please to heal him or take him home. I let go of telling you what to do. Thy will be done." Soon after I prayed that prayer, the hospice worker came to see Greg and I told her what I had just done. She told me I did the right thing and I felt sad yet comforted by her encouragement. But then I needed to tell Greg what I had done. I was so scared because up to that point I kept trusting God for his complete and total healing. Now it looked like I was giving up all hope. Greg had told me earlier that we were in a spiritual battle and he told the Lord he would be his front man no matter the cost. He then challenged me if I was going to sit on the sidelines or jump into battle and fight the good fight as well. I had told Greg that I would trust God and fight the good fight as well and believe with him for his total healing. Those words lingered in my mind. Was I now giving up the good fight or was it right to let go and surrender to God and His will? Strange as it may sound, I felt a huge weight lifted off my heart when I let go and let God decide what He wanted to do with Greg's life.

After the social worker left, I made the courageous walk into our bedroom and told Greg what I had just done. As I expected, he was very upset with me thinking I had given up all hope for his healing. I cried as I left his bedside. During the whole time that Greg was in bed in severe pain, he would ask me for three things. One was to play the Bible on tape for him so that the Word of God would fill his heart and mind during this time of intense battle. Second, he wanted me to play soft praise and worship music to quiet his heart and to put him in a state of continual worship. The third was the hardest for me to do. He asked me to sit by his bedside and read the scriptures to him while he slept or rested. Sitting there and watching him suffer nearly broke my heart. I also selfishly would think of all the things that needed to get done. Being with him, however, was truly the most important thing. When I would leave his bedside, I would listen for his moans. I knew he was in severe pain when he cried out "Jesus, I praise you, Jesus, I thank you, Jesus, I love you." I would immediately run to the room and he would tell me what he needed. Oftentimes it was more pain killing medicine. We had a wonderful doctor on staff at the ministry and all I had to do was call him and either he or his nurse would come over and bring more IV pain medicine or whatever Greg needed to relieve his suffering.

He Was There All the Time

Our pastor had told me earlier in the day that he wanted to come over that night to pray with Greg and bring him holy communion. Greg was looking forward to this special time with our pastor. But when he came, we didn't expect to hear what he had to say. He had no idea what had happened to me earlier in the day so the timing of this was surreal. He began by saying" "Greg up until now, I have stood with you for your healing, but I think the Lord has other plans and I think He is calling you home to Himself." I could not believe my ears! Was this a confirmation of what I had done earlier or what? Then I heard Greg's final words: "OK, pastor" and with that, he closed his eyes and went immediately into a coma. I cried as I watched my beloved husband totally let go himself and surrender his final hours on this earth to the Lord and His will for him. He never did receive communion. The Lord, however, was preparing him for a real face- to-face and heart-to-heart communion with Himself.

Thanksgiving Day was a very sad day for us as a family. Greg was in the next room in a coma and you could hear a pin drop around our table. The food was wonderful, but we could barely eat. We all wanted to cry as we said our good byes to my husband, my children's wonderful Daddy and our good friend. Word spread that Greg was dying, and friends came over to pray and let him know he was loved. His students came by and I could see the tears well up in their eyes as they too said good bye to a good friend who loved and believed in them to the end.

The next day, the doctor came over and said it was now just a matter of hours. Greg's body was slowly shutting down. By night time, the children and I were at his bedside and I started hearing soft, beautiful music coming from our living room. When I went out to see who was there, the room was full of friends singing beautiful hymns. They sounded like a choir of angels ushering Greg into his eternal home. The guitarist came into our bedroom and played softly for Greg as well. What a homecoming this was! It was all so spontaneous as well. None of this was planned by man, BUT GOD decided to pull a group of wonderful Christians together to send their brother home in an angelic way. I could never have asked for such a beautiful homecoming.

As Greg was coming near the end of his earthly life, our doctor said it was time for everyone to leave our bedroom and quietly slip away so that the children and I could be with him alone at his bedside. I cried hard when our son Joey said "Daddy, Daddy please don't leave us." The children and I all sobbed as he took his last breath. By this time, it was almost midnight. We walked out of our bedroom as we awaited the hearse to come, a very broken family. The kids adored their father and I had just lost my best friend. How could we go on, I thought? Greg was such a strong Christian man and anchor for our family. He humbly lived

He Was There All the Time

what he preached. We needed him, and he was now gone. Our son was 14 and the girls were 16, 17 and 18.

The next day was very hard for me when I had to go to the funeral home to pick out Greg's casket and make his final arrangements. A friend went with me for moral support but only by God's grace and mercy was I able to make it through such a painful ordeal. Once again, however, I had another profound experience with the Lord. In the mist of my excruciating pain and suffering, I thought to myself how wonderful these people are to me. I then thought I want to pass on to others, Lord, what you are doing through them for me, at my time of loss. For some very strange reason, I felt like I would love to work in a funeral home someday and pass on the love and care I received. Little did I know at the time that this would come to pass in a most unexpected way years later!

Post Mortem

The next several months were simply unbearable for all of us, to put it mildly.

Our oldest daughter was attending bible school on the ministry's campus when Greg died, so thankfully, she was nearby. But she too suffered this great loss. After she had finished bible school, she began teaching 5th grade at our Christian ministry's school. After school, however, she would go to her bedroom and not talk to anyone. After completing her year of teaching, she decided that she wanted to earn her college degree. She also thought that she might want to serve in the military, so she applied for an ROTC scholarship at the same school that had accepted her; however, before signing the scholarship papers, she decided that a future life in the military was not for her. She eventually went on to earn a degree in linguistics with a minor in English.

He Was There All the Time

Our youngest daughter was a senior in high school when her father died. She wanted to attend one of our country's military academies and Greg had encouraged her to do just that. She was grieving in her own way, all the while under tremendous stress, trying to finish up her senior year and filling out applications and being interviewed by our congressman's selection committee. In order to receive an appointment to one the service academies, she needed our congressman's recommendation. By God's grace she eventually was accepted into West Point. Although Greg was not around when the good news came, I am sure he was smiling down on her from heaven.

Following his father's death, our son had a very hard time in high school keeping his grades up while still suffering deep emotional pain. He spent all his free time on his skateboard or playing video games. My heart broke for him, as I saw his life going nowhere. He lost all interest in school and had no desire to go to college. He needed to be doing something constructive with his life. I encouraged him to perhaps think about joining the military, just to give him a purpose and direction in his life. During his senior year in high school, he decided to enlist in the US Marines Corps. But the pain persisted, as it did with his sisters.

Our special needs daughter took Greg's death very, very hard. She and her dad were very close. In fact, he was the only one that she would mind and not give a hard time to. She simply adored him. At the time of Greg's death, she was living in the women's group home at our ministry so that her needs would continue to be taken care of while I tried to get myself strong again. She too suffered deeply, and I believe the effects of her father's death eventually caused her to start having major seizures.

So many emotions erupted after Greg's death and I thought I was going crazy some days! What made it even worse was to watch my four children suffering and I did not even feel I had the strength or ability to comfort them because of my own grieving. I felt like an unfit mother. As much as I tried to reach out to our children, I knew I could not take away their pain. I could only be there beside them and carry the load together in the strength of the Lord.

I would go to work and barely be able to function. I was teaching third grade which I loved, but I would find myself starting to cry at the drop of a hat. I began to ask the Lord what I should do. I knew I had to make a change but to what? Then a thought came to me. I think I need a very easy job that would not require a lot of preparation or stress. As I thought about the various jobs at the ministry, the one that jumped out to me was the laundry. I loved washing and folding clothes at home so why not do it on a much bigger scale? I debated about telling my principal that I needed to change jobs and the one I felt was right for me was the laundry! I decided to pray and leave it up to the Lord! One day, the assistant principal came to me -- and seeing what a wreck I was -- said lovingly: "We think you need a change of jobs for now." I could not believe my ears when she told me that they wanted me to go to the laundry where the stress would be a lot less and that the environment would give me time to grieve and heal. It's absolutely amazing what happens when we leave our struggles with the Lord. Perhaps it was Him who put the whole idea of going to the laundry into my head so that I would be ready to let go of the job I loved.

During this time, I also was so burdened with all the paper work involved with Greg's death and trying to care for my children and myself. I felt like we were all being pulled in different directions and I just did not know which way to turn. I felt like my head was in a heavy fog and I could not think straight. But then two very strange things happened to me on two different occasions. I felt they were both visitations from Greg. I believe the Lord saw my heart pain and permitted Greg to visit me in a very unexpected way.

One night, while sound asleep, I had a very powerful dream; however, I would rather call it a vision because it was more than a dream. In this vision, the children and I were in an airport waiting for someone and then as I looked off, I saw Greg approaching us and he looked healthy, radiant and so joyful. I had never seen him look so happy. He had a big smile on his face as if he was thrilled to see us all again. He walked over to us and gave each of us a big hug and the kids were thrilled to see their daddy again. No one wanted to let him go. He told us how happy he was to see us again. Then I heard him say he had to leave us and go back to where he came from. And we all started to cry and beg him not to leave but he said he had to go back. As he left, he changed from being a man who we could touch and hug into a spirit and he got bigger and bigger and bigger as he drifted and floated away like a vapor. I actually could see through him as he drifted back through the wall from where he came. Then I woke up! I cried wondering why I had such a powerful vision. The only thing I could think is that the Lord wanted me to see that Greg was healed, happy and healthy and waiting for us on the other side.

On another occasion, I was very worried about many financial issues especially my oldest daughter's college tuition. I had other financial burdens beyond my ability to pay as well. I just kept saying Greg "I wish you were here to help me with all these trials I am now facing alone." I felt so scared, lonely and afraid of the future. Then one night it happened again. I had another visitation from Greg, but it came in a very different form. I woke up from a sound sleep and I heard his voice say to me: "If you only knew Jesus the way I now know Jesus, you would never have another worry in the world again." I remember thinking: "Then please Greg, help me come to know him like you now know Him!" Little did I ever dream how this was going to come to pass later in my life! As I look back on this difficult time, I now know why the Lord put

He Was There All the Time

on my heart that we keep the life insurance policy on Greg. When we purchased the insurance, he was in good health. When times were difficult for us financially, he was ready to cancel the policy, but I felt in my spirit that we needed to keep it. Little did we ever dream, that shortly thereafter, he would get cancer. God's ways and thoughts are higher than ours!

In the months that followed I cried, sobbed at times, dried and ironed clothes and sobbed some more. I wondered if the sobbing would ever stop! Sometimes, I would go home after work and just pound the floor and scream just to let all the pain out. Barely able to hold myself together, I felt awful that I could not be a better moral support to my children. I criticized myself for being a weak Christian and mother who could not stand up under such stress.

As time went on, I started getting physically sick with severe stomach pain due to stress. I could barely eat and lost a lot of weight. I recall a very low point, when one day while at work in the laundry room, I received a call from the principal that my son was having a major meltdown (much like my own!) and that he was being sent over to me to help comfort him. My heart melted when he walked through the door and fell into my arms sobbing and sobbing. We held each other tight and cried together. Again, I thank God for the caring principal, teachers, and staff who allowed us this time to just be real and to heal.

I thanked God that I lived and worked for a wonderful ministry where I knew my disabled daughter's needs were being well cared for also. I knew she wanted to be home with me, but I could not take care of her many needs and mine too. One day, a woman from her group home called and said she had found her on the floor in her bedroom having a severe seizure. She was now laying lifeless on the floor, so they recommended my taking her to the small, local, community hospital for evaluation. The nearest hospital was about an hour away, and without thinking clearly, I just grabbed her and off we went. My daughter was in a deep unresponsive state and nothing was bringing her out of it. When we arrived at the hospital, several tests were run but she continued to remain in this state for several hours. After having done everything they could, the emergency room doctor recommended that she be taken by ambulance to a big city hospital for further testing. While being evaluated at the big city hospital, my daughter did eventually come out of the unresponsive state. However, she was confused and not talking clearly. She did not remember anything that had happened to her. It was just the beginning of another health issue in her life: seizures! Perhaps, this was her body's way of grieving this deep loss. Each of us was suffering in a very different way.

After Greg had died, our children and I all agreed that we could not stay in our big beautiful home. The memories were too painful

He Was There All the Time

plus it was too big for me to care for. Our family had dwindled from six to three with my special needs daughter living in the woman's group home and my youngest daughter at West Point. My oldest daughter was getting ready to go off to college as well. The big question came: where were we to go? I prayed hard and asked the Lord to give us a smaller home that would be right for us. It just so happened that I heard about a family wanting to move from their small home to a bigger home. I approached them and asked if they might be interested in swapping homes. When they checked out our home they loved it and agreed to it. When I saw their home I immediately fell in love with it and just knew it was the right place for us too. With approval from our pastor, we made the swap with few problems. In the move I decided to give back most of the furniture that was loaned to us. Many people had gotten together to fill our big home when we had returned from China and now this furniture did not fit into our much smaller home. It was time to start all over again. It was painful but fun as we picked out new furniture for our "new home!"

Something changed after we made the move and started settling into our "new normal." I used to hate getting my hands soiled in the dirt. Greg loved gardening and I would sit on the curb while he did all the planting of beautiful flowers and digging up weeds. He would always encourage me to join him, but I told him I just didn't want to get dirt in my nails. I know it was an excuse, but I hated bugs too! I just was not a gardener! But something miraculous happened when we moved into our new home. The front yard desperately needed a huge make over and there was no one to do it but me! In tears, I wished I had listened to Greg and learned how to garden because now I needed his help more than ever, yet he was no longer here. But God had a plan unbeknownst to me! I never dreamed the help would come in the way it did. A friend brought us some manure to help me get started. I then prayed hard and went to a garden center to buy soil and plants. When I arrived there, I did not know where to begin or what to get so I asked a gentleman in the garden department to help me. He was wonderful, and I thanked him for helping me get started on this new venture. When I went to thank him, I noticed his name was "Greg." Was this a God incident or not? I could not help but think that Greg was looking down on me from heaven and that God had sent this Greg to help me in place of my husband.

Through many tears and hard work trying to break up very hard clay, the flowers were finally planted. As the months rolled by, I discovered it was fun getting my hands dirty, pulling weeds and watering my beautiful flowers each day. I could not believe this was me! Perhaps this was my husband's way of helping me to heal from heaven.

He Was There All the Time

Although I was having fun caring for my flowers, I still felt a very deep pain in my heart. I started working other part-time jobs just to keep even more busy. I enjoyed working a few afternoons a week in the cannery canning vegetables and fruit. It was a very relaxing job. I also was a weekend receptionist a couple of Saturdays a month. During this time, however, I started developing severe arm pain along with my IBS stomach pain. When I told my doctor about all my symptoms, he suggested that I go on an anti-depressant to help me cope with the grief. I told him that I did not want to go on meds again. I had done that years before and I just wanted to feel the pain and just struggle through it with the help of the Lord.

At that time, our pastor was planning a mission trip to Israel and I really wanted to go because I was desperately searching for answers. Oftentimes I would sit in the ministry's cemetery where Greg was buried and ask him and the Lord what to do next in my life. I knew I had to take care of my special needs daughter, so I could not think of going back to the mission field. I wondered if I should stay at the ministry or leave. But where would I go? A friend gave me a little recorder and he told me to just go to the gravesite and pour out my heart to the Lord and record it. It felt weird, but I did just that. It became clear to me that even though I felt so sick, I needed to take this trip to Israel. I never dreamed how powerful this trip was going to be and the life changing affect it would have on me.

While in the Holy Land, we saw many of the famous religious sites; some of them had quite a profound effect on me. The Lord spoke to my heart on several occasions in ways I did not expect or even want to hear! For example, there was a church next to the Garden of Gethsemane in Jerusalem -- the Church of All Nations. As we walked into the church, there were two Franciscan monks standing in the doorway. I then heard these words: "You too are a Franciscan." I thought to myself: What?" But I let it go. On another occasion, we visited Our Lady of Mount Carmel near Haifa, the home of the Carmelite sisters. While we were there, we visited their little chapel with votive candles you could light. For some strange reason, I felt like I was supposed to light a candle, but I did not want to do this in front of my pastor and other Protestant friends. That was a very "Catholic thing" and I did not want them to question or ridicule me! I waited until everyone had left the chapel and then I quickly went over and lit a candle. When I turned around, there was one of my friends who just smiled at me and did not say a word. We then went outside and there was a little garden area with the statue of our Blessed Mother. I saw myself drift over to this area while others were looking at the other sights. I then did something I had not done in years. I said a prayer to Mary asking for her help! I was so desperate I was willing to do anything.

But there was an even more profound encounter with the Lord. Our pastor took us to the Garden Tomb, which many Protestants believe is the burial place of Christ, not the Holy Sepulcher. It was a very beautiful, peaceful park with lots of foliage and flowers…and an empty tomb cut into the rock. I could not wait to go see it. Once inside, I did not want to leave. It was cold and stark just like my emotions. There was a bench outside the tomb which I gravitated to after my visit. I just sat there and stared at the empty tomb asking the Lord where He was in my life. I felt so dead and lifeless just like that tomb and I did not know where to turn for answers. I was praying, reading my Bible, going to church, trying to live a good Christian life but I just felt nothing but spiritual numbness in my heart. While sitting on that bench I had a heart-to-heart talk with the Lord and I begged Him to come into me in a deeper, more intimate and more profound way.

I then added a second petition. I prayed, "Lord, I loved serving you in full time Christian ministry with my husband. If it be your will, could you bring another wonderful man into my life so that we together can serve you once again?" As I was finishing my prayer, someone from our group came over to get me to take me to a nearby gazebo for a communion service that our pastor was having. As I sat in that gazebo, I noticed a huge rock that looked just like skull hill. For a second, I went into a trance and thought to myself that I feel just as dead and lifeless as that skull. Then I heard our pastor say: "Body of Christ" as he went around to each of us. But when he came to me something very strange happened in my heart. When he put the communion in my hand, I said to myself "I can no longer just have a memory of you, Lord. I have to HAVE YOU!" Then I heard these words spoken so gently and tenderly: "Come back to Eucharist." I started to cry because I knew it was the Lord speaking to me, calling me back to the Catholic Church. In my heart, I said to Him angrily I will never go back to that church that hurt me so badly as a young person. After this incident, I felt very depressed, confused and scared. Was this really the Lord who spoke to me or was it my imagination? I really felt like I might be going crazy!

When I returned from Israel, my life went from bad to worse. I made a very poor decision one weekend and decided I needed to get away, so I went to a nearby town to spend the day with a friend and stay in a hotel for the night. I loved this hotel because it held many happy family memories.

While sitting at the pool, I started to hallucinate, and I literally saw in my mind's eye, my husband and children all swimming in the pool and diving for pennies. I heard their laughter as they cried: "Daddy throw me in the water." They were all so happy and the incident was so real it scared me. Then I came to and realized it was all a mirage and not real at all. That sent me into a very deep downward spiral of despair as I tried to numb my pain. Instead of going to this once happy place for refreshment, I came away more broken than ever before. BUT GOD had a very special plan which was soon to unfold. He was going to use all this brokenness for His highest glory and my greatest good.

I thought I was going insane because of all these recent experiences in Israel and at the hotel. Soon after, I ended up in the emergency room with severe bodily pain. When the doctor checked me out he said he could find nothing wrong with me. He then asked what I was going through and I told him. He was a very compassionate man and he then went on to say that he saw me in a very dark tunnel and that God had a very special plan for my life and I would soon be seeing the light at the end of the tunnel. I could not believe what I was hearing. This doctor was speaking hope and life back into my soul. Was he an angel unaware? Of all the doctors, I could have seen that very day, God sent this man to minister to my very wounded heart. I held onto his words as if they came from Jesus Himself! Perhaps they did!

When I returned home, I visited my own doctor and told him of all the severe pain I was experiencing. When he saw the hospital reports, he suggested that it was not physical but emotional problems with which I was dealing. He suggested I see a Christian psychiatrist in a city, two hours away. I did not want to do this, but he told me the man was a very good Christian and that he probably could help me. I reluctantly decided to go see this doctor.

When I met this doctor, I immediately broke down crying as I shared all that I had been through with my husband's death, the pain of loss and the voices I heard in Israel. I told him how I felt the Lord was calling me back to the Catholic Church and how scared I was to come back. I told him about the abuse I had experienced when I was young. I just laid it all out for him to see. I feared he was going to tell me I really was a crazy woman! Instead I saw him smiling as I poured out my painful life story! I could not help but wonder why he was smiling at me. He did not appear shocked or amazed.

He then went on to tell me his story. He said that he had been raised Catholic and that he grew up in the same city as me and he even went into the seminary to become a priest. While in seminary, he discerned that the priesthood was not for him and that marriage was. He then went on to tell me that he eventually left the Catholic Church and that he had counseled many priests over the years. He totally understood the abuse issues I had encountered as a young woman. He told me to be very careful when counseling with priests -- to be sure of their motives, something I was not aware of as a young woman. He told me that they had problems just like all of us. He then went on to say that I was not to expect my friends to understand that God could be calling me back to the Catholic Church. He further went on to say that he felt I was truly hearing from the Lord and I should be sensitive to His voice and obey if that is what I felt He was calling me to do. He finished by saying that I was not crazy at all. I went to him twice more and that gave me the courage to get out of the boat, go forward and to "do it afraid."

During this intense time of searching, I was praying hard, reading my Bible and talking to the Lord openly and honestly. One night I heard His voice again. He said: "Go out to the garage and look in Greg's memory box for his rosary." I said: "What? Why?" Again, I thought I was going crazy but the next day I went out to the garage and pulled the box off the shelf, opened it up and sitting there was Greg's rosary (probably from the time of His First Holy Communion) as if it was waiting to be found! Once found, I asked the Lord what He wanted me to do with it. After all I didn't know how to pray the rosary; moreover, why was I supposed to pray it. I also thought that if my son saw me with the rosary, he would wonder what his mother was up to. I tried to hide it from plain sight. Not knowing what to do, I decided to call my brother and tell him what was going on in my heart. I shared with him that I felt the Lord was calling me back to the Catholic faith and that He wanted me to pray the rosary; however, I did not know how or why. My brother e-mailed me the instructions and I immediately started praying it. The more I prayed the rosary, the more peaceful I felt.

It was like a natural tranquilizer, as I meditated on the life of Jesus. I could not believe the effect praying the rosary was having on me during this very turbulent time in my life.

As I continued to seek the Lord about my future, I asked him if I should look for a priest and find out how to return to the Catholic Church. We were living in the Bible Belt and there were very few Catholic Churches around, so I did not really know where to go. I prayed, and the Lord told me one day to open the phone book and go to the yellow pages, which I did. I saw two Catholic Churches listed in the nearest city -- which was about 50 minutes away. Nervously, I picked up the phone and dialed one of the numbers. A kind lady answered the phone and I started out saying that I know you probably think I am a crazy woman and I probably am, but I had an encounter with the Lord in Israel and I think He is calling me back to the Catholic Church. I asked her: "Do you know of a good priest who can help me return after 25 plus years of being in the Protestant Church?" She said that her pastor was very good but she also knew of a wonderful priest who was retired from his university teaching position but who would be just excellent for me; however, she also told me that he was quite sick. I asked her if she could call him for me and she readily agreed. Later, she called me back with his answer. "Of course, I will help her, he said, as long as she needs me. I will be here to help her return to the Catholic Church."

He Was There All the Time

Father JJ was a gem. He was a very kind, sensitive elderly priest, who had helped other people from other Protestant backgrounds enter – or in my case, return to the Catholic Church. What a match made in heaven! This truly was a God incident! Once again, only God could have brought this about especially because there were so few Catholic churches or priests in our area. He was a very holy man that I could totally trust with my life. I sobbed as I made my very long confession and he lovingly embraced me with the tenderness of Jesus. I felt so accepted and loved by Him and the Lord. He would tell me to go to the university adoration chapel and just lie on the floor and let the Lord heal me. He said just rest in His presence. Don't read, pray or do anything. Just be with the Lord and let Him heal your very wounded heart. For months, I did this as I continued to pray and discern the Lord's will for me and my future. As time went on, I would tell Fr. JJ what the Lord had done in my life and what I felt He was telling me to do in the future. He told me that I was a "mystic" but that it was important that I not get ahead of the Lord when He would show me things that would be happening in the future. He told me to always go slow and pray and ask for wisdom and discernment and to keep talking to the Lord, which I did.

Also during this time, other strange things were happening as well. For some time, someone had been sending me a copy of the *Marian Helper* magazine, published by the Marians of the

Immaculate Conception in Stockbridge, Massachusetts, but when it came, I always threw it away saying it was Catholic and I did not want to have anything to do with Catholic literature. But on one occasion, I heard the Lord speak loud and clear: "Do not throw this magazine away. I want you to read it!" I did!

In this particular issue, there was a story about a Polish Catholic nun who lived in the early 1900's. Jesus would appear to her in visions and talk to her. Her name was Sister Faustina. I was captivated by her story and was shocked to think that a Catholic could talk to Jesus -- and that He answered her! This nun had a very deep and personal relationship with Jesus (like me) and this really surprised me. As a Protestant, it was very common to hear people say that the Lord spoke to them. In fact, that is where I learned more fully to really hear the voice of the Lord speak to my heart. I was taught how to contemplate and meditate on the Lord's words in Holy Scripture and learn to just be quiet in His presence and listen to His still small voice. Now I was reading about a nun who had similar experiences as myself. This absolutely fascinated me, and I wanted to learn more about her. I contacted the Marians in Stockbridge to send me St. Faustina's meditation book based on the words that Jesus had spoken to her. After that, I wanted to read her diary of *Divine Mercy* to learn more about her. I could not believe that the Lord sent this wonderful nun -- St. Faustina -- to me in a cornfield in the Midwest to help me find my way back to the Catholic Church! I felt like I had a good friend and that I knew her, and she was sent to be my mentor.

During my lunch break at work, I often would go off by myself and pray this prayer that Jesus gave her and focus on this picture of Him with two rays coming from His heart representing His blood and water. The pale rays reflected His forgiveness of my sins and the red rays His filling me up with His life. I did not understand what I was doing at the time. I simply and naively would pray this Divine Mercy prayer and I would feel such peace after doing it. I really could feel the presence of Jesus. I did not understand that, at that time, real graces were coming to me from heaven, as I prayed this prayer. I only felt the wonderful effects as I said: "Jesus, I trust in you."

Along with St. Faustina, the Lord sent me another friend. In a subsequent issue of the *Marian Helper*, there was a wonderful article about a Marian priest -- Father Don Calloway -- and his unbelievable conversion into the Catholic faith. I read the article about his book, *No Turning Back,* and I knew I had to read it. I immediately sent for the book and devoured it like a starving child. Once again, I could not believe a person could have this kind of conversion into the Catholic faith! I had seen all kinds of people having conversions to the Lord in the Protestant faith but never to the Catholic faith. This just stunned me. Was the Lord using St.

Faustina and Fr. Calloway to bring me lovingly back to the Catholic Church?

Perhaps the psychiatrist was right and that the Lord was calling me back and that I should listen to His still small voice and just take the grand leap and just "do it afraid." But where was I to go? My son was preparing to leave for the Marine Corps and my two other daughters were away at college. The woman's home had come to me and said that I needed to bring my daughter back home to live with me again. I was very safe and secure in my Protestant ministry. I had a beautiful home with brand new furniture, a good paying job, a wonderful pastor and church, and excellent medical insurance.

As I continued in intense prayer, I heard the Lord say to me one day out of the blue: "Return home to take care of your elderly parents." Dad had had a stroke and was now in a nursing home and Mom lived alone. I had no idea how this would work out. I would have my special needs daughter with me, so I had to think carefully and prayerfully about this situation. As I was praying about this possibility another very strange incident happened. One day, my special needs daughter and I were driving to the airport to pick up my West Point daughter who was coming home for a few day's visit. Out of the blue she said to me: "Mom have you ever thought of leaving the ministry here and going back home to be with grandma and grandpa?" I couldn't believe the timing of her question and that it came from my sensitive special needs daughter! Out of the mouth of babes came wisdom and confirmation! Soon after, I took the leap of faith and called my mom. Sheepishly I said: "Mom, I am coming home" and she excitedly said, "When are you coming home to visit?" I replied "No, Mom, it's not for a visit; it's for good -- to help you out if you need my help." She then started to cry and told me that she had been praying to God to send her an angel to help her and that I was that angel sent in answer to her prayer. My mom was a real prayer warrior and God heard her prayer and put it not only on my heart but my daughter's too!

As I started thinking about all the practicalities of the move, I felt overwhelmed until one day I heard the voice of the Lord again. He said: "Go and sell everything you have; give to the poor and come follow me; do not be afraid of tomorrow for I am already there." Later, He added: "For eye has not seen nor ear heard the things I have for you if you but trust and obey." I knew that the Lord was speaking those words to me and I took them to heart. Sometime after that He said: "I am calling you to be an evangelist to my wounded hurting people." I did not quite understand that, and I said "But Lord, I am so wounded myself. How can I give what I don't have myself?" But He did not answer me.

During this time, I continued to seek medical help for the physical pain I was experiencing. I learned that I had a cyst and was told that I should keep a close watch on it. But I did not want to do that, so I opted for surgery. After the surgery, I stayed at our ministry while healing; however, I began thinking about the move back home. I struggled with having to give away or sell all our beautiful new furniture. I struggled with how I was going to talk to our pastor to tell him I felt the Lord was calling me home to care for my elderly parents and to come back to the Catholic Church. I struggled with having to give up a good job, a ministry, insurance, security, and safety for my daughter. I really wondered if all of this was the Lord or just me imagining that I had heard from Him. But I had all these confirmations, so how could I have missed the mark? Following the Lord is truly a walk of faith and child-like trust and I felt like a child who was walking blindly hand in hand with our Lord. Finally, I decided not to question or doubt any longer but just believe! God said it, that settles it, I believe what He told me to do, so now I must simply and humbly obey. Amen. So be it.

I was uncertain what my pastor would say when I told him I was leaving the ministry. He was so sweet when he said that it was right that I go home and care for my elderly parents; however, he was very concerned for my daughter's well-being. I agreed with him, but I told him that if God was calling me, He would help me care for her many needs as well. I told him I had to just trust God and do what He was calling me to do. He blessed me, and his words gave me the courage to leave the ministry and all its security behind and just "do it afraid!"

It was a bitter sweet departure as I said good bye to our beloved pastor and the many people who had become family to us over these many years. But I knew I had to obey the Lord and just do what He was calling me to do.

I Did It Afraid

I'm Coming Home, Mom

The next year proved to be a severe trial for my mom, my daughter and myself. My mom had an extra bedroom in her home, so she invited us to move in with her. I went from a nice sized home to a small bedroom that my daughter and I both shared. While living with mom, she became quite sick with pneumonia and was hospitalized on several occasions. She also suffered from severe depression like the days of old when I was growing up. She would want all the blinds down and the room dark and I just hated that. It brought back very painful memories of my childhood. She was grieving the loss of her husband not being by her side. It pained her to see that he was not getting the best care he deserved in the nursing home. She lived in a beautiful home, but it meant nothing to her. She just wanted her husband back and that was not meant to be. In fact, after the stroke, my dad started to suffer from dementia and thought that I was his wife and referred to me as such. It was very sad and painful to see my once robust dad acting like a little child. It was even more heart breaking for my mom.

Not only was mom having her own emotional and physical health issues, but she was having issues with my daughter's behavior. They were like oil and water. My daughter could never do anything right. Mom wanted her home to be perfect and neither of us could live up to her standards. She would get so upset with us, especially my daughter. It got to the point that after several months of living with her, I had a little "meltdown" and was seriously considering moving out. I even found a great place for us to live but when it came time to put a deposit on the apartment, the Lord convicted me. He said: "Why did I call you home? Was it not to care for your elderly parents? Now take up your cross instead of trying to dodge it. Do not run away from what I have called you to do." I quickly repented and asked Him to give me the strength and love I needed to care for my parents until He saw fit to take them home. That meltdown occurred in October, eleven months after I had moved in with my mom.

One day, as I was struggling with how to handle this whole situation with my mom and daughter, the Lord spoke again very clearly to my heart: "Strive to be at peace with them, overcome evil with good and it is more blessed to give than it is to receive." Whenever I felt that I was between a rock and a hard place or losing my patience, I would say these words out loud to remind myself of the Lord's words to me. To this day, I still say these words when I am dealing with a difficult person or situation in which I do not know how to respond.

The previous summer (prior to my little meltdown), I had another encounter with the Lord. One day while praying in my bedroom, I felt I heard the Lord speak to my heart again. He knew of my desire to be happily married and serving Him again someday in joint ministry but that sure didn't look likely now. He said: "I am going to send someone into your life and that person is going to be a very strong devout Catholic who is going to help you grow in your Catholic faith and you are going to help him learn how to walk in the spirit." I recall arguing with the Lord saying, "No, Lord that is not what I want! I want to marry someone who is Catholic, but walking in the spirit also, like I had done these many years as a Protestant." He did not answer me, and I totally forgot about our conversation that day.

When I moved back home to care for mom, I attended a very good Protestant Church with my daughter on Sundays, but I kept thinking about the Lord's call to me personally. I knew I had to find a good Catholic Church, but I did not know where to go. I recalled that the church I had grown up in was very liberal and I did not want to go back there because it was liberalism which messed me up so many years ago. I really wanted a very orthodox church where I would continue to grow close to the Lord as I had as a

He Was There All the Time

Protestant. One day, out of the blue I heard the Lord say: "Go back to the church you grew up in because it is not the same as when you were a young person." I argued with the Lord, but I finally decided to go. I joined a women's bible study group which really helped me grow in my new found Catholic faith. I could not believe how much this very "liberal" church had changed! My bible study teacher then told me about a prayer group that focused on the Bible and St. Faustina's diary. She thought I might be interested in joining that group as well. I could not believe it. That truly was another God incident. I started going to daily Mass and staying afterwards to pray the rosary and the Divine Mercy Chaplet with a small group of daily church goers. God truly did lead me to this wonderful church that had radically changed – for the better -- from the time I was there in the 60's and 70's.

I continued to grow in my faith. One day, in October, while sharing my reversion story with the people who attended this prayer meeting, the woman in charge told me about a Catholic woman's prayer breakfast that was held every few months in our diocese. A speaker would share her testimony on how God had been working in her life. She thought I might be a good speaker at one of their upcoming meetings, so she put me in touch with the woman in charge.

When this woman, who headed up the Catholic woman's prayer breakfast heard my story, she asked if I would be willing to be their speaker the following May. I was humbled and honored, despite the challenges I was facing at home. This chance meeting occurred around the same time the Lord convicted me to lovingly die to myself and care for my parents without complaining. I was feeling like such a failure as a Christian because of the situation with my mom and daughter. The timing was surreal. How could anyone want to hear my story knowing the struggles I was dealing with, in my own family? I felt so unworthy, but I decided to trust the Lord and, "do it afraid." Once I quit fighting the Lord and accepted my cross, I felt peace re-enter my soul as I said: "Lord, I will lovingly care for my mom and dad and daughter for however long you decide. Your will be done."

On December 8th – the Feast of the Immaculate Conception -- this women's group was having its prayer breakfast and I decided to go so that I would know what to expect in May when I was to share my life story. After the meeting was over, there was a time for prayer, so I asked for prayer for myself. I told one lady that I wanted to be married again someday and there was a good friend I liked but he was a former Catholic who was not at all interested in returning to the Catholic faith. The lady said, "Did you ever think that God might have someone else in mind for you?" I said who would ever want to marry an older woman who has a disabled special needs adult child that I need to care for. Also, I was caring for my elderly parents, as well. She said," Why don't we pray and trust the Lord to bring the person He has in mind for you rather than what you think is best." I agreed to pray and afterwards I felt such faith grow in me as if it was a done deal. I felt such peace as I let go of my desire.

One evening, unbeknownst my prayer request at the breakfast meeting, my mom asked me, out of the blue: "Why don't you call Marvin." My sister was there so she heard this same conversation. I said: "What Mom? What are you talking about?" She pursued the issue and said: "You know, the man you dated in college. You can probably find him on the internet." I replied: "Mom he is a very happily married man and I am not in the business of breaking up marriages." With that, I stormed out of her room and went to my bedroom. I then prayed to the Lord and said: "Lord, if I am ever to get married again I would want it to be to Marvin but I will never go looking for him. If you want me to marry him, you will have to bring him to me and then I will know, beyond a shadow of a doubt, that this was truly your will and not mine." After that, I totally forgot about this whole bizarre incident.

During this time, I recall telling my brother, one day, that I thought dad would live for many years despite his dementia and other health issues. He just seemed to be existing and it was very heartbreaking to see him like this, but we saw no radical changes in his situation. Then something DID CHANGE! He suddenly started going downhill and the nurses got concerned. It was getting close to Christmas and mom became sick and ended up back in the hospital with pneumonia again. It was the Wednesday before Christmas and a decision was made to call in hospice for my dad. When I talked to the ladies from hospice they said that they thought dad probably would live at least to February. Having been through this with my husband Greg, I did not think he would live that long. By Friday, however, his body was shutting down and we knew we had to tell mom what was happening. We went to the hospital to get her released so that she could be by her beloved's bedside. As sick as she was, she was his faithful partner and wanted to be with him until the very end.

Saturday was Christmas Eve and we all surrounded his bedside as he lay there so peacefully and unconsciously. Mom held his hand and just before he took his last breath she said lovingly and tenderly: "John, John we have done everything together for 61 years. Now let's do this together too, but please ask Jesus to make sure I am ready before He calls me home." With that He breathed his last. It was so painful to watch my mom say good bye to her beloved husband whom she absolutely adored.

Christmas Day was another awfully painful holiday which brought back memories of Greg's death at Thanksgiving time just five years earlier. The next few days were not easy as we prepared for dad's funeral.

He Was There All the Time

On Monday, the Lord spoke to my heart again. He said: "Go get your haircut because you are going to see an old boyfriend at the funeral home visitation." I made a joke of it and said: "Yeah Lord. I had dated a lot of guys while growing up and I wondered which one would I see, if any of them?" I called my sister and asked if she could come over and stay with mom while I had my hair cut. She agreed to it but when she arrived at my parents' home that night I said: "No! I am not going to go. I've change my mind." I really thought this was not the Lord but my imagination speaking to me. My sister, however, insisted that I go. She said that she had driven all the way out there, now I needed to go get my hair cut! Having not told her why I was going to get my haircut, I quietly went.

Wednesday – the day of dad's visitation -- was a very difficult day for mom, as well as for the rest of my family. Many people knew my dad because he was a well-known business man in our area and very active in many inter-denominational Christian organizations. Many people flocked to the funeral home and it was packed for several hours. As the oldest child, I stood in the receiving line and greeted people while mom, in her very weakened condition, sat on a chair next to Dad's casket with my sister standing behind her to support her.

I did not know most of the people, but I graciously thanked them for coming. Then the unexpected happened. A gentleman walked up to me and said, "Cheryl, do you know who I am?" I looked at him and I said: No, I don't think I know you." He replied: "I am Marvin." I almost fainted when he told me his name. He looked so different from when I had dated him in college some 37 or so years prior to this encounter! I embraced him, and he later told me that I hugged him so hard that he felt faint. Immediately I wondered where his wife was because he appeared to be alone. He told me that he was very sorry about dad's death and my own husband's death. He then went on to say that his wife had also died suddenly of a heart attack, almost seven years ago. He said that he was home visiting his mother for the Christmas holiday and he happened to read the obituaries in the local newspaper and saw that my dad had died -- and that I was a widow. I was holding on to his hands as he spoke. Again, he later told me that I held his hands so tight that he was losing feeling in his fingers.

I told Marvin that I wanted to take him to see my mom. At this point he had no idea why I was saying this. Little did he know what had happened just a couple of weeks prior to dad's untimely death. When he saw mom, he bent down before her and extended his condolences and said: "Almost 40 years ago you and your husband opened your home to me and Cheryl opened her heart." Without batting an eyelash or missing a beat, my mom responded: "Marvin!" She couldn't believe it any more than I could. My sister, who was present when my mother had talked about Marvin two weeks previously, shouted: "Oh My God!" I felt that everyone in the funeral parlor was looking at us.

As we both kneeled to pray before my dad's casket, a memory went back to my days of youth when Marvin and I had dated. Dad loved Marvin and wanted me to marry him, but I was not ready because of my unresolved issue about being a missionary. But here we were at dad's side and I thought that dad had brought us back together through his unexpected death while mom prophetically spoke him back into my life. If the hospice workers had been right in their calculations regarding dad's death, my meeting Marvin would never have happened. I could not help but think that this was truly another God incident. As crazy as it sounds, I guess I did hear from God when He said go get your haircut because you are going to meet an old boyfriend! However, I never dreamed it would be Marvin as we hadn't been in touch for almost four decades.

Another strange thing happened, after my Dad's funeral home visitation. I was visiting some friends and the wife asked if I knew the date of my dad's wake. I told her I could barely remember what day it was let alone what date his wake was held. She then went on to say that it was my wedding anniversary, December 28th. Then a strange bizarre memory came back to me. When Greg was very sick and in the hospital, he told me -- in front of a good friend of ours -- he knew that God was not done with me. He

I Did It Afraid

went on to say that God had more work for me to do and that He was going to bring another man into my life. I remember crying and saying: "No Greg, no Greg, please don't say that!" He then turned to our friend and said to her: "Please remind my wife of these words after I am gone." Those words were piercing at the time but here I was kneeling in prayer at dad's casket thinking about dad and mom's blessing. Now I couldn't help but believe that on our wedding anniversary, I also had my husband's blessing as well! This was too surreal for me to wrap my head around! Was this all a dream, a mirage or was God really orchestrating all these strange events? Only time would tell.

I invited Marvin to the funeral Mass the next day – Thursday -- and the luncheon but he was not sure if he would come as he was leaving for home on Friday. I was so blessed when he did show up. When we arrived at the restaurant, I really did not know how to act. I was so terribly nervous feeling like a teenager on her first date! I knew I needed to sit by my Mom and care for her, so we sat Marvin with my cousins who remembered him from many years ago! My sister, however, came to me and said that there was one extra seat next to Marvin and she encouraged me to go sit with him while she cared for mom. When I sat down next to him he said: "Would you like to break bread together?" and I nervously said yes. I remember him saying that when we used to date. I felt like no time had passed between us and yet over 37 years of life had gone by in each of our lives.

I invited him to come over to our home afterwards to catch up on each other's lives. The hours flew by like minutes as we shared our life stories. It was a wonderful reunion and I wondered what God had in mind from this very unexpected event. He went back home to Virginia and I continued to care for mom. After the luncheon, Mom went home to bed but never recovered. Two days later, we called hospice and they told us that she was very close to death. She had been quite sick for a while and I believe that she stayed alive just to be by her beloved husband until his passing. Then she felt ready to go home herself. What a very beautiful love story. Two days later Mom went home to be with her beloved Jesus and her husband. I was blessed to have my Divine Mercy prayer group come over and join me in sending her home with the Divine Mercy chaplet. It was another beautiful homecoming.

A New Beginning

After Mom's passing I started praying as to what God had for me to do next with my life. I really did not know where God was leading my daughter and me. I just took it one day at a time. My oldest daughter was finishing up her college education, majoring in Linguistics, and my son was in the Marine Corps. My youngest daughter had graduated from West Point and was dating a young man who graduated from the Naval Academy. They met when he was an exchange student at West Point. Upon graduation, he decided he wanted to be a Marine helicopter pilot. My daughter knew in her heart that they were going to marry someday so she went before a committee at West Point requesting that she cross commission to the Marines. They granted her request and after graduation she went straight to Quantico for her Marine training. It was strange visiting her at

He Was There All the Time

Quantico, my old stomping grounds, never dreaming one of my children would be there someday.

A few weeks after my Mom's passing, Marvin and I started corresponding. I typically wrote him very long snail mail letters and he would respond to them by sending me much shorter beautiful e-mails. Before Marvin came back into my life, I had made plans to go visit my daughter at Quantico. It was no coincidence that Marvin's home was nearby! I would be able to visit Marvin while visiting my daughter as well! I really believe that God had it all planned before I knew what He was up to!

Marvin and I had wonderful conversations and lots of fun together. But he had some serious decisions to make because he already was in a relationship with another woman. I was not aware of this at the time. As time went on, we both started noticing that something was happening between us. Our conversations got more serious as we discussed our situations.

He knew about my need to care for my special needs daughter and he wondered how that would affect our relationship. He had a very good friend who had an intellectually disabled son and he told Marvin how challenging it would be. Nevertheless, Marvin felt he could handle it. We seemed to be weathering each difficulty as they arose.

One day, however, I got a call from Marvin saying that we had to break it off because he did not think he really could handle my situation after all. We said good bye -- once again. Only this time it was him breaking it off and not me! I told him with a lump in my throat and a very broken heart that I totally understood as we parted, once again good friends. My heart was broken but I would never have forced him to accept my challenging situation. It had to be the Lord's will if it was going to work. I cried and felt sad inside, but once again I said: "Lord thy will be done."

The next two days were very sad for me and I felt this empty void return to my heart. Marvin had filled a hole that brought me so much joy but now I had to let him go and accept God's will in all of this. I kept saying: "Lord why did you ever bring him back into my life in the first place?" But I did not receive an answer.

Two days later, very early in the morning, I received a phone call that woke me up out of a sound sleep and it was like music to my ears when I heard Marvin's voice. He said that since we "broke up" he was miserable, and he prayed hard about our situation and he did not want to break up after all. With the Lord's help, he wanted to trust the Lord to give him what he needed to love me and help care for my daughter. It was not at all an easy decision, but it was one that only he and the Lord could come to. I had to stay totally out of it or it could have been disastrous. It had to be purely God's will and not mine if it was going to work at all. What brought about this change of heart for Marvin was a song he heard the day before while attending the children's Mass at his church. It was a song by the *Weston Priory* and included the words: *"Come back to me with all your heart. Don't let fear keep us apart. Trees do bend though straight and tall so must we to other's call. Long have I waited for your coming home to me and living sweetly our new life."* What perfect timing! We both saw this as God's way of saying to Marvin: "You have my blessing. I will give you the strength and the wisdom you need to care for this woman and her special needs daughter -- and her other children as well."

Our relationship continued to grow with the help of the Lord. Time was flying by as I was looking so forward to Holy Week, my favorite time of year. It was soon Holy Thursday and a friend asked me if I would like to join her and a group of other people from our church to visit seven different churches around the city. We would travel by bus to these different churches and say a prayer and move on. I told her that I never heard of doing this, but I was open to the idea if I was not working that night. What grabbed my attention was the possibility that we might see an "empty tomb" at one of these churches. I did not quite understand what that meant but I told her how God spoke to me in Israel at an empty tomb, to come back to Him in Eucharist and how that was the turning point in my life. The empty tomb was not at all empty to me because the risen Jesus had brought me back to Himself and the Catholic Church in a very profound way. I prayed and said: "Lord if this is something you want me to experience, please do not let me be scheduled to work that night." My daughter also worked so we both had to be free to do this. I was not even sure if she would be open to the idea if we both were free. But once again God had a divine plan and both she and I were free, and she was willing to go! I was so excited. I could not wait, hoping that we would see an empty tomb in one of these churches!

As we approached the sixth church, I was so disappointed that we had not seen an empty tomb in any of the beautiful churches we had visited that evening. It was getting quite late and as we pulled into the parking lot of the church my phone rang and I could not imagine who would be calling me this late. I debated if I should take the phone out of my purse and see who it was. My daughter said: "Oh Mom, just answer it." When I did, I heard Marvin's voice and I was so glad that I did answer my phone! He said: "I have a hypothetical question for you. If I were to ask you to marry me, what would your answer be?" I told my daughter what he said, and she said: "Mom you better say yes!" I quickly said: "Of course the answer is yes!" And that was the end of our conversation.

What happened next is even more amazing. When we walked into this beautiful church there near the altar was an empty tomb!!! I ran up to it and started to cry in utter thanksgiving over what had just happened. The living Jesus had answered my twofold prayer

He Was There All the Time

that I cried out to Him just two years prior when I stood outside the empty tomb in Israel. I had asked Him for two things. First that He would come into my heart in a deeper and more intimate way and He did answer that prayer by lovingly calling me back to Holy Eucharist and to His wonderful, Catholic Church. He had already done a remarkable healing and I now loved my church and the people who once had hurt me. He helped me to forgive those who had wounded me so many years earlier in my life. He also helped me to see that we are all frail, broken people in need of His love and mercy. He showed me that, although people are flawed, His church is not.

Now to my utter amazement, He had just answered the second part of my prayer. I had prayed at that empty tomb that, if it be His will, He would bring another wonderful man into my life so that we could serve the Lord together as husband and wife. What incredible timing that just as we were pulling into this very church parking lot, I should get a call from Marvin asking me if I would marry him? How surreal is that! I knelt before my Lord in utter child-like thanksgiving over what He had done and was continuing to do in my life. I had to pinch myself to feel if this was all real or just a dream.

Before this event, Marvin had invited me down south to his nephew's wedding the weekend after Easter. I was excited to be visiting him again. It was Friday the 13th, a very special day for my dad, who – if you recall – survived a plane crash when he was in the army on Friday the 13th. I previously had told Marvin why this day was so special to my dad. Never did I dream it was going to be my special day as well. Again, I felt like dad was smiling down on us and giving us his blessing on this, his lucky day. Marvin invited me to morning Mass at his church and I was very happy to be joining him to celebrate the Lord's supper together. I was also very happy to hear that his church had an empty tomb as well! I could not wait to see it and when I got there I immediately went up to it and prayed hard to know for sure the Lord's will for us. I wanted to know that God was really leading us and not me.

After Mass was over, Marvin invited me to join him at the empty tomb. As we knelt there, he said, "Cheryl, two years ago you stood outside an empty tomb in Israel and asked the Lord to come into your heart in a deeper and more personal way and He answered your prayer by bringing you back to Eucharist and the Catholic Church. Today I want to answer the second part of your prayer. Will you marry me?" and with that he proposed and put a beautiful ring on my finger. Again, I was in awe. Could all this be happening to me or was it just a dream? The next day we went to his nephew's wedding. At the reception, I caught the bouquet and Marvin caught the garter. The bride came up to me having never met me and told me that she knew that Marvin and I were meant for each other, yet we never told anyone of his proposal to me the day before. We did not want to take away from their wedding, so we were going to make the announcement sometime later.

Soon after, the announcement was made to our families and friends, and a wedding date needed to be set. Marvin suggested that we plan a June wedding. It was late April. That meant only two months to plan and pull it all together. But we both had done this before – planned a wedding on very short notice! In both of our first marriages, we had very short engagements and were married in just a few months. But this was a summer wedding and most places are booked at least a year in advance. But once again God had a plan!

I had called several places and, just as I expected, everything was booked up. There was one hotel, however, that had an opening if we were willing to have our wedding reception in an outdoor tent. I agreed to check it out. When I arrived at the hotel, I realized that this was another God incident. I used to take my Mom to the beauty salon that was on the property of this very lovely hotel. While she was in the beauty salon getting her hair and nails done, I would sit outside at the picnic table and pray my rosary. One Saturday while praying, I looked over at the parking lot and saw a beautiful bride getting out of her car and walking into the hotel. I remember thinking how I wish that could be me someday but that sure did not look probable due to the calling that God had placed on my heart at that time. My call was to be present to my parents and my special needs daughter and take care of their needs. Quickly I went back to praying and forgot about this secret desire known only to God. I could not believe that this was now the same hotel that mom used to get her hair done! Could Mom have been a part of this plan to have an opening occur on the very day we wanted to be married at a hotel where I dreamed of having my wedding someday? Again, this was all too amazing. Marvin checked out the hotel and we both loved the idea of having an outdoor wedding reception in its backyard overlooking the beautiful grounds, with vibrant summer flowers and gorgeous foliage! It was truly like being in paradise! Only God could have put this together for us!

Next came the wedding gown. I only had two months to find the right gown and, being that I was getting married in the Catholic Church, I wanted to wear a beautiful white gown and the Lord once again led me to the right place and the right gown. The store even had its own photographic service, so we did not have to go looking for a photographer. Everything was falling into place as if heaven had planned this wedding and we were just going through the motions.

But everything was not perfect with my children unfortunately and this caused me a great heartache. My special needs daughter struggled with my getting married once she realized what was happening. My oldest daughter tried to convince me not to get married and my son knew nothing about my dating a man, our short engagement and now marriage. He was at sea. My youngest daughter, however, was very happy for me that Marvin had come back into my life. She thought he was so good for me! My heart was torn, and I kept asking the Lord if this was all Him or just me. How could I feel so at peace and torn at the same time? As hard as it was, I decided to trust God, and, once again, just "do it afraid." I had to obey God and follow where He was leading me no matter the cost. My only desire was to please and honor Him and the cost was great, but I had to go forward and trust the outcome to Him.

With the flurry of activities preparing for our wedding, the women's prayer breakfast in May came upon me quite quickly. I was very nervous about sharing my return to the Catholic Church and Holy Eucharist. Would I be accepted, or would people reject my story because of all the suffering and pain that I had been through? Once again, I had to leave the outcome to God. I went forward and just "did it afraid". After the meeting was over, a lady came up to me and said she too had serious problems with members of the Catholic Church and was about to leave but after hearing my story decided to stay! If it was only for her, I thought the cost of being vulnerable about my past was worth sharing.

I could not believe that just five months earlier I had attended this very meeting and a lovely woman prayed with me that God would bring someone into my life to serve the Lord together in ministry and here I was with my husband to be! My memory also drifted back to the previous summer when the Lord had spoken to me one day in my bedroom saying that I am going to bring a man into your life who is a very devout Catholic and he is going to help you grow in your faith. You in turn are going to help him learn how to walk by the spirit. Now I was sharing with others how all this was coming to pass just as the Lord had said it would! Others came up and thanked me as well for my openness and honesty at which point I gave all glory to God for giving me the courage to be vulnerable. We just never know whose lives are being touched when we share our broken wounded souls and God's loving mercy upon us in our struggles with others.

June 23rd came very quickly, and the day was perfect. It was very warm and sunny; it could not have been a more beautiful day for our wedding. It was wonderful to be married in the very church that I grew up in and that the Lord had brought me back to after much healing. I rejoiced as we exchanged our wedding vows as well as afterwards, bringing a beautiful bouquet of roses to MaMa Mary who had been my constant companion and help through my journey back to the fullness of faith in her Son and His church. Again, I looked back on our first encounter at Mount Carmel in Israel and how, through her powerful intercession, I was now standing before her, thanking her for all she and Jesus had done for me. I was in a cloud of heavenly bliss that day.

My dear sweet Divine Mercy friends gave us a beautiful afternoon reception afterwards and once again my memory streamed back to St. Faustina and the major role she too had been playing in my life as well! She led me to this wonderful group of humble servants who also loved the Lord and loved sharing His Divine Mercy with others. I recalled thinking how hard it was to leave my safe, secure, wonderful Protestant ministry and the people who had become my family for years. But the Lord assured me that if I left it all behind, He would go before me and lead me and my family gently by the hand. As scared as I felt at the time, "I did it afraid" and trusted Him to lead me, which He did! I just could not believe that I was now part of a wonderful Divine Mercy family serving the Lord and His people in the Catholic Church. Once again, I was just blown away at how awesome God really is!

When Marvin asked me where I wanted to go for our honeymoon I did not have to think twice about the answer. I immediately said I want to go to the Marians of the Immaculate Conception in Stockbridge, Massachusetts to thank the Lord, His Mother Mary and St. Faustina for bringing me back to the Catholic Church and to Divine Mercy and His Presence in the Holy Eucharist. Since reading St. Faustina's meditations, I started reading more of the books that this ministry published, and I just wanted to share with the Marians how God used their ministry to bring me home to fullness of faith, especially in the Holy Eucharist. In their magazine, Father Mike Gaitley was mentioned and I personally wanted to meet him and share my story on how his ministry and St. Faustina brought me back to the Catholic Church.

God went before us once again and opened the door for us to meet Fr. Mike. I had prayed that if it be God's will, we could meet him because I had read about him in their magazine. Sure enough, he was in his office the day we visited but in a hurry. He told us he only had a few minutes as he was getting ready to go to a meeting. Quickly, I started to share my reversion story with him and as he became more interested in hearing it, he canceled his meeting. We spent well over an hour with this "divine appointment." He encouraged me to write and share my story with others.

He Was There All the Time

A New Life

As I continue my story from this point to the present, it is not written in consecutive order of events. Many of these events have occurred at the same time and many continue even into the present.

When we returned from our honeymoon, we immediately moved to Marvin's home in Virginia. Life was not very easy. My special needs daughter was living with us and it was an adjustment for all of us to now become a "family." Marvin had never had children and I had four adult children, so this took some major adjusting on all our parts. It became very stressful and so many times I found myself crying out to God as to why it was so difficult. I knew in my heart that He had called Marvin and I together, but I did not know life was going to be so challenging for all of us. Lots of tears were shed as we walked through some very trying days. All I could do to quiet my heart was spend time in adoration and say: "Jesus, I trust in you" when nothing made sense. Marvin also introduced me to the Divine Mercy Cenacle group at his church. Immediately I found a home among these wonderful believers. We met every other week; however, this was not enough for me. I wanted to be a part of a Divine Mercy cenacle every week to help me grow more deeply in my Catholic faith. Therefore, I joined another Divine Mercy group at a neighboring Catholic church.

I also met a woman in our church who has a weekly prayer meeting in her home. I love going to her prayer meetings where I have seen God work mightily in my heart as well as others. I have seen many healings and miracles take place as well during these prayer meetings. My Divine Mercy Cenacle meetings -- along with this prayer meeting -- have become a very important part of my spiritual growth and still are to this day. This woman also heads up Christian Women in Action (CWIA) a ministry which has a bi-monthly prayer breakfast like the one I spoke at, just before we were married. When she met me, she too asked me to share my story at one of her prayer breakfast meetings. I have stayed actively involved with CWIA as well.

Soon after we were married, my oldest daughter went to Poland to teach English to pre-school children for a year. After that, she came back to the United States and has lived in our area working at various jobs. My son finished his four year commitment with the Marines and has returned to our area to go to college. My youngest daughter is now married and serving in the Marines with her husband.

As mentioned previously, my special needs daughter was having a very hard time living with us the first couple of years because she wanted to be independent and live on her own. Her behavior started to get more and more out of control and once again I cried out to God for help. I felt like we were between a rock and a hard place and I realized that Jesus is the rock, so I turned desperately to Him for answers. We had placed her on a waiting list to get an Intellectual Disability (ID) waiver which would entitle her to live in a group home and receive the many services she needed; however, she was on a ten-year waiting list and there were well over 8,000 people before her, waiting to obtain this waiver! But this was nothing for God! He could move mountains and that is just what He did! When her case worker saw how difficult things were getting for us at home, my daughter was moved to a "more urgent list" with over 2,000 people. Then, one day, I received a very unexpected call from her case worker telling me that she was being moved to a critical list of just 20 people and that out of that 20, only four would receive the ID waiver.

We went into intense prayer asking for the Lord's will to be done for her. We only wanted what was best for all of us and we did not know what that was. The miracle came! She was one of the very few selected to receive the next waiver. We knew that God had moved heaven and earth to make this impossible situation happen. With the help of her case worker, she was placed in a group home about 60 miles away. Unfortunately, things did not work out there, and we prayed hard to find her another home.

Marvin had found a Christian group home on the internet, so we checked that one out and she seemed very pleased with that choice, so we moved her there. Her personal needs, however, were not being adequately met to her liking. The staff was very patient and wonderful, but my daughter wanted to move out of a group home setting. Once again, her behavior got out of control. She insisted that she wanted to live with a family instead. Her case worker found a program that places intellectually disabled people in families. She is living with a wonderful family at present and is adjusting quite nicely.

About a year after we were married, another God incident occurred. Marvin and I attend daily Mass. One morning, while standing outside the front door of the church talking with some friends, a vehicle from a local funeral home arrived to deliver flowers for a funeral later that day. Marvin opened the doors of the church for the two men whose hands were full of floral arrangements. When they came out of the church, Marvin once again opened the doors for them. They joked with Marvin that he should come work with them. We asked if, in fact, they were hiring, and they said yes! Soon after, I was telling my cousin about this incident. I told her about the wonderful care I received when my husband died and how I wanted to do the same for others in that same situation. If given the opportunity, I wanted to pass the blessing I received onto others. She encouraged me, saying that if you feel God is giving you this divine ministry opportunity, go for it!

Very nervously, I went to the funeral home and a very lovely lady came to the door. She was the owner's wife. I told her the whole story about meeting two of their employees at our church. I further told her that they told us that the funeral home was hiring, so I was interested in applying for a job. Shortly thereafter, I met her husband and subsequently was hired as "a greeter" – the individual who meets and greets mourners at visitations.

I just loved my ministry "job". Memories went back to my own husband's death and the feelings I had when I was making his arrangements. At the time I felt like I wanted to help others in this same situation someday. Was it the Lord who planted that desire in me some time back? It had to be because I absolutely loved my job and saw it as ministry and not a job. I felt humbled and blessed to be able to minister to other wounded, hurting souls. I could totally relate to what they were feeling and going through.

During that time, I would work many nights alone answering the door or phone when there were no visitations. While praying, I

He Was There All the Time

would feel a sweet presence in the building. One night I felt I heard the Lord say that if only I could see the huge angels floating around. I could feel their presence in a very real way and the Lord also told me that He and His mother were there as well. One day, another employee asked me if I ever felt like there were spirits floating around here at night when I was alone, and I told her yes! I thought perhaps I was going crazy thinking these weird thoughts. I mustered the courage to ask some priests about it and they said it was not surprising at all to them and to simply cover myself with holy water when I was at the funeral home. But what was even more strange is that when I would greet people at night who came for viewings, many people would tell me that they felt that our funeral home was so different than any other funeral home that they ever had been to. They felt such a sweet peace there. I would smile knowing it was because the Lord was present in that place and even strangers felt it.

After working at the funeral home for about two years, I started getting rumblings in my heart that my days were numbered and that the Lord was getting me ready for something else. About two months later, due to unexpected circumstances, that proved to be the case. I was saddened to leave, but I knew it was the Lord's timing to do something else.

One Sunday about two years ago, before Mass began, I went to the back room behind the sanctuary to use the restroom when suddenly I had another one of those out of body experiences like I had when I was 18 years old. My body left my body and I saw a vision and heard the Lord's voice speak tenderly to my heart. In the vision, I was standing at the foot of a huge cross and Jesus was looking lovingly down at me while His Mother was cradling Marvin and I under her mantle on her right side and my four children and daughter's husband were cradled under her arm on the left side. Then I heard Jesus tenderly speak to my heart: "Whenever you don't feel loved just come back to this place." With that, my body returned into my body and my eye sight returned and I felt like someone had just lifted a heavy weight off my heart. I felt so loved and whenever I pass that very spot I recall what happened to me that day. At the time, we were going through some intense struggles and I wondered where the Lord was in all of this. That day He reminded me that He does stick closer to us than a brother, even when we don't feel His presence. He truly is there all the time.

Divine Mercy Sunday was very different for me this past year. I felt the Lord say that this was going to be a different Sunday from past Divine Mercy Sundays that I had celebrated. I heard Him say: "Go! Now! I am calling you to be my Ambassador of Mercy to share with others this message of Divine Mercy with the world." He showed me that while St. Faustina was working from heaven, I would I be working with Jesus and her here on earth. He was calling me to be His hands and feet, to bring other wounded souls into His Church hospital to receive the same love and care I had been receiving these past several years. When the Lord spoke that word to me my response was: "Yes!! Amen, Lord, I am your handmaid be it done to me according to your Word."

Over the past year something else has been evolving in my heart with which I have struggled. I started noticing some women wearing veils at Mass. It reminded me of when I was a child wearing a mantilla. I thought it was a nice gesture, but I sure would not want to do that myself and stand out. Pride was gripping my heart. I did not understand why women did this except perhaps out of reverence for our Lord. Then something started happening in my own heart. I felt like the Lord was asking me to do the same thing and for months I fought Him. I did not know why He wanted me to do it and He did not tell me why either. He just lovingly invited me to do it. I kept thinking what are other people going to think of me? Will they think I am trying to show off and act like I am holier than thou? Internally, I battled with the Lord for quite some time until one day I finally said: "OK Lord, thy will be done. I don't understand this old-fashioned custom but if you are asking me to do this I will surrender and obey." My next question was where do I go and get one of these lovely veils? I felt foolish asking one of the ladies again because of pride! Then out of the blue something very strange happened one early morning. My husband and I pray the Liturgy of the Hours with a few friends every morning before Mass. I turned to one of the gentlemen that we pray with and said I think I want to start veiling but I do not even know where to acquire one. His immediate response stunned me when he said that he had just seen in our local Catholic newspaper an advertisement for veils! Who would have thought that this man would have the answer to my need? I saw this God-incident as a sweet gift from the Lord.

When he gave me the information, I called the ministry that makes beautiful veils and I shared my story with the lady who answered the phone (Veils by Lily.com). She was very kind and helped me understand that we veil out of deep reverence for our Lord in the Eucharist. I ordered a few veils and she told me that she would enclose some information to better help me understand the depth of meaning behind veiling at Mass. As embarrassed as I felt about doing this, I was also very excited to step out and obey the Lord and just "do it afraid". Little did I know what was going to happen once I died to my pride and just focused my attention on HIM and not what others thought of me!

One day, after Mass was over, I noticed something when I removed my veil. I felt a cold breeze on my shoulder and neck. Yet when I put this very thin veil on, I felt a warmth cover my neck and head. After reading the pamphlets explaining why we veil, along with this experience of warmth when wearing the veil, the

He Was There All the Time

Lord spoke to my heart that the veil was His covering over me. When I veiled I felt His love, mercy and protection. He felt so very close to me and I felt so safe and secure as if He were holding me in His arms. I read that the veil serves as a tabernacle for the Lord and when I wear it, He and I become one -- He in me and I in Him! When I veil, I can feel it! I feel so connected to my Lord in a deep way! He showed me that while on earth we are separated by a thin veil so we walk by faith in His presence but once we die, we will see Him face to face. Somehow when I wear my veil I feel that heaven has come down and removed the veil between us and I become one with my Lord in Holy Eucharist. It's much deeper than just reverence for Him; it's now intimacy and oneness with the King of Kings and Lord of Lords. Little did I ever dream what the Lord had in mind when He lovingly asked me to veil. Oftentimes, we need to just obey when nothing makes sense, die to pride and just "do it afraid!" not caring what others think!

Reflections of My Journey With the Lord

As I reflect on my life story to this point (it never really ends), I sit back in awe over the things that the Lord has done in my broken, wounded life. Jesus is still in the miracle business, making something beautiful out of our messed-up lives if we only let Him have total control. But I must totally surrender daily everything (including my sins and weaknesses) and everyone I care about to His merciful love. This is exactly what He wants from us. The scary part is just letting go, not knowing what will happen yet with childlike trust and confidence submitting to the Holy Spirit saying: "OK Lord, your will be done no matter the cost or consequences." I need to choose (with God's help and an act of my will) to let go of trying to protect myself or others from pain or suffering and say: "Jesus, I trust in you for the process and outcome." This is not easy but oh so freeing when I do it. I am finding out that my worst enemy is Satan. He works through the world, my circumstances, others and my flesh. Pride, vanity and wanting to be in control are my arch enemies -- walking in the Spirit versus walking in the flesh. I like to keep my feet on the ground, always, knowing where I am going and when and how I am going to get there. Fear of pain and suffering have a way of paralyzing my heart as well. But let me emphasize that Jesus says that He comes to give us life and give it abundantly, but we must let go of ourselves and our preconceived ideas about ourselves, others and circumstances. Satan comes to steal, kill and destroy along with keeping us in fear, worry, doubt and anxiety about everything! (See John 10:10)

It's a daily battle of spiritual warfare and not a walk in the park. The battleground is truly in the mind. Every day I keep reminding myself to listen to Jesus and His still small voice and not the lies of Satan who condemns me for every sin and mess up I have ever committed. He'll tell me I am no good or he'll have me compare my life to that of others. He will tell me that my present sufferings are due to my sinful past and a consequence I must live with, the rest of my life. Jesus, on the other hand, tells me to give all my weaknesses and sins to Him and He will make something beautiful out of them (see Romans 8:28). What Satan intended for evil, God will now use for good to spread His kingdom, mercy and love. Satan is a liar and he is full of lies trying hard to use my sins against me to bring me to despair instead of hope in God's mercy.

I love that phrase "Oh happy fault (blessed fall) that merited such and so great a Redeemer!" I love the verse from Jeremiah 31:3 where the Lord tells us: "With age-old love I have loved you, so I have kept my mercy toward you." Verse 4 says: "Again, I will build you and you shall be built." How beautiful that no matter how broken or messed up our past is, the Lord loves us personally and unconditionally and wants to build us up into the wonderful person He created and destined us to be so that we can love and serve Him and others. We simply confess our sins and our need for Him as our Lord and Redeemer and let Him do the rest. What love!

The Bible tells us to take captive "every thought" and bring it to the obedience of Christ. (See 2 Corinthians 10:5). With all vigilance guard your heart, for in it are the sources of life (See Proverbs 4:23-27).

As I look back on my life, I see how deceptive Satan has been and how he lied to me. I bought into those lies from the time I was a teenager. "Don't trust God with your life. He wants to withhold the desires of your heart. Don't let any man tell you what to do including God. Be your own "god" and do it your way." Little did I know that doing it *my way* led to deep sorrow, pain, regrets and consequences. I thank God, however, for His son Jesus, who is there ready to pick us up with His mercy and clean us up when we fall deep into the pit that Satan lays before us.

He Was There All the Time

I see in my mind a deep, deep pit made of miry clay (See Psalm 40: 2-3). I see myself in that pit with no way out or up unless the Lord from above lifts me up by His arms of love and mercy. That is what He is continually doing in my life. He has shown me over and over that no pit of sin, pain or suffering is so deep that His mercy, forgiveness, healing love are not deeper still. I can never earn His love or do enough to make Him love me. He just simply says to gaze on Him on the cross and see that "this is true unconditional love!" It's all about Him and not me! When I gaze upon Him crucified, I feel so loved even though I know how dirty I am inside. I just keep hearing the words: "Be not afraid my child to come to Me. My love and mercy will clean you up; not reject you!" I just simply cry out to Him asking for His forgiveness for being so stubborn, rebellious and hard-headed as well as hard-hearted.

When I sit at Mass and gaze on the crucifix, I see all my sins on Him. My life flashes before me and instead of feeling hopeless and despairing, I hear Him say: "My beloved child come to me, I am waiting here for you. I love you and want to heal you and show you the life I have planned for you. My plans for you are good ones and you will have no ill consequences only blessings upon blessings upon blessings if you will just trust and obey." (See Jeremiah 29:11-14)

Looking back on all the things that the Lord has asked me to do in my life, I think the hardest thing has been for me to write my life story. I have had to "do it afraid." Jesus is asking me to be real, transparent, vulnerable and share my brokenness, defects and woundedness with others so that they may be healed and set free and come into a deep and personal relationship with Him as well. It's not about religion but about relationship. As a child, I had religion, but I did not know the God that I worshiped. He was austere, strict, scary and very far away. I feared going to hell if I badly sinned. Then as I grew older and fell into deeper sins, I began to feel hopeless and despairing. That led to self-rejection because I did not live up to my very prideful "goody-good religious self" that I came to be known by. Sinful acts became a stronghold that temporarily numbed my deep emotional pain and longing for true, unconditional love. How could God really love and accept me and how could I love and forgive myself? It has been much harder for me to forgive myself than those who have hurt me! That is pride. If the God of the universe can forgive me, who do I think I am that I cannot forgive myself!

Most of my life I tried to be that perfect Christian that everyone thought I was but inside, I knew I was not. I was addicted to needing people's approval to feel loved and I would do anything they wanted just to feel their love. But Jesus in His mercy continues to help me break through that perfectionistic addiction and the lie that I believed about myself and to see myself as I really am, a child of His, in need of His mercy, forgiveness and grace. That is both very frightening and very freeing.

What has been most scary to me is the fear of rejection by those whom I love or who love me. Many of my sins and strongholds have been known only to God and me. Satan works in the dark and he loves for us to keep our sins in secret rather that confessing them to Jesus through a priest in confession and getting set free from them! Jesus, on the other hand wants us to walk in the light as He is in the light and be free to be who He intended us to be! I now see that the strongholds are like a salve that we put on a deep wound. It might numb the pain for a while, but the pain keeps resurfacing. I realize that our wounded hearts were created by God to be filled by Him with His love.

For me, in the past, I used to fill my heart with pleasing people, honor, prestige, good jobs, and sexual impurity. God, however, makes clear in the Bible, especially in His 10 Commandments, what things are pleasing to Him and what things hurt Him in our relationship with Him and with others. As a society today, we don't look to these Commandments as a gauge for loving Him first and others and ourselves next. We are truly free when we do everything out of love for Him and others and not out of self-centered love. In Acts 5: 29 Peter says: "We must obey God rather than men" and this goes contrary to what people are saying these days. It takes strength, moral courage and humility to live for God and walk in His ways. To live for God today is to go against the tide, but we must ask for the strength to live courageously and show people the way to God and to true freedom and peace.

Revelation 12: 9-11 refers to Satan as the deceiver, the accuser of the brethren, who has been thrown down to earth and he accuses us day and night before God. Yet we have conquered him by the blood of the lamb, Jesus, and the word of our testimony, for we love not our lives even unto death. Therefore, we need to share what God is doing in our lives and how He is changing us and helping us to walk in holiness. Jesus is the lamb that died for our sins to forgive us and to save us from God's wrath. He is our advocate who stands between us and God like an attorney. We are all guilty of sin and no one can stand before God and get into heaven in a sinful state. But Jesus has taken all our sins, condemnation, shame, guilt and consequences onto Him on the cross and nailed them there. When God sees us, He sees Jesus standing there between us and Him and through His death and blood shed on the cross, we are saved, provided we turn to Him for forgiveness and mercy. This is the message of Divine Mercy that God gave to St. Faustina.

Now is the time of mercy, as Jesus told St. Faustina before the great and terrible day of judgment that the Bible warns us about. See James 2:13 which says that mercy triumphs over judgment.

2 Corinthians 5:10 says "For we all must appear before the judgment seat of Christ, so that each one may receive recompense, according to what he did in the body, whether good or evil." Salvation is an ongoing day-to-day experience wherein we continue to listen to God's voice and choose to obey Him and do it God's way rather than listen to our own selfish desires, impulses, passions or affections. We daily choose to submit our very selves to Him and walk in His ways.

We teach best by modeling what we are learning from the Lord. We need to help each other get to heaven! This is good news that our world desperately needs to hear. That is why the message of Divine Mercy is so powerful. We need to see ourselves and others through the rays of blood and water which pierced Jesus's heart on the cross. We need to pray the Divine Mercy chaplet over ourselves and all others because we are all in need of His continual graces that flow from His heart, pierced for us. Jesus desires that we all walk in the victory He obtained for us on the cross of Calvary but how often do we even think of the price He paid to save our souls from death? Now is the time to reach out to His merciful heart and ask Him to help us to really know Him and what He longs to give us as His beloved children. So often we suffer needlessly because we do not know the living God who longs to have a loving, personal relationship with us.

Many people -- Catholics, Protestants and others -- need to hear this good news too because Satan is out to deceive even the very elect. Hosea 4:6 says that my people are ruined for lack of knowledge. That is why we need to read God's Word and put it into practice, everyday so that we can be set free from the lies that society teaches us.

The Bible says that our bodies are not our own. (1 Corinthians 6:19) They were bought at a great price – by the blood of Jesus -- therefore we must respect and regard our bodies with great dignity and never abuse ourselves or others through sexual immorality. We are God's children made in His image; therefore, we must always do things to bless and edify and encourage each other, not hurt or wound each other through abusive, negative, hurtful or even sarcastic words or actions. Our body is the temple of the Holy Spirit. God lives in us and that is why we must be sure that we work to keep our hearts, souls and bodies clean and pure and teach others by our word and example how to live holy lives pleasing to God. Living this way leads to freedom and peace within ourselves and with each other. (See 1 Corinthians 6:12-20).

Recently while focusing on the crucifix at church, Satan, the accuser of the brethren, tempted me with thoughts of shame, guilt and condemnation over my past sins. He said I was now suffering severe physical pain because of my past sins and that God was now punishing me for all the ways I had offended him. Then, suddenly, I saw a rushing river in front of me and I heard the Lord speak lovingly and tenderly to my heart that my sins were washed away as far as the east is from the west (See Psalm 103: 10-14) and I saw that river flowing from the cross! He assured me that what has been confessed and repented of is now washed away, never to be brought up again. The Lord then went on to say that I was to offer up my physical pain and suffering to Him and unite it to His suffering on the cross for my own sanctification and continuing salvation and for the conversion and healing of others. My pain now had a purpose and not the one Satan threw up to me! What freedom and peace came to me. We are truly in a spiritual warfare and Satan wants to drive a wedge between us and God and His love and mercy for us. He also does not want us to be honest with each other and help others to heal and come to know Jesus as our merciful God who is here to help us live holy lives and help us get to heaven. In my moments of temptation, like this recent one, I immediately run to Jesus and Mary and cry: "Help, please set me free from these tormenting lies and temptations." Jesus promises that with every temptation, He will give us a means of escape if we turn to Him and do whatever He tells us to do (See 1 Corinthians 10:12-14).

As in the example of the wedding feast of Cana, when our wine runs dry, He wants to fill us with the best of His wine. All we need to do is listen and do whatever He tells us to do. Just obey. (See

John 2:3-5). I am learning the more we desire to be close to Jesus, the more the enemy is going to try to pull us away through all kinds of temptations, lies and deceptions -- but he can not do anything that the Lord does not permit him to do. The Lord allows us to be tested to strengthen our faith. We realize that we are only little children in this big world of His and we are helplessly dependent on God for everything. Faith says: "OK God, this situation is too big for me to solve. I simply surrender this difficulty to you. Thank you in advance for taking care of it in your will, way, means and timing. Amen." We must daily exercise our faith muscle, or it will grow weak. As we use it, we become stronger. The Bible says: "He must increase and we decrease." (See John 3:30). Faith in God means depending on Him -- not ourselves -- to do the impossible in our lives and that of others. We cannot save ourselves or set ourselves free of addictions, strongholds, emotional pain, the temptations of the world, our flesh or the devil. We need God and His mighty power to do for us what we cannot do for ourselves! All we need to do is call on His name, repent of doing things our way and He will come to us quickly because He loves showering us with His mercy.

As Jesus told St. Faustina: "Now is the time of mercy." Come to Jesus and be fed. Drink from His well that never runs dry or turns rancid or leaves you with regrets, pain and sorrow. Isaiah 55:1 tells us: "All you who are thirsty, come to the water! You who have no money, come buy grain and eat." Verse 2 goes on to say: "Why spend your money for what is not bread; your wages for what does not satisfy." Yet we do this all the time by trying to fill our hearts with the things of the world. He waits patiently for us to return to Him.

I want to share the words of a song the Lord gave me many years ago when I was suffering from severe clinical depression and chronic pain. At the time, I was feeling a sense of hopelessness and despair, thinking I would never get better. I had just poured out my heart to the doctor, and as I was driving home from his office, these words suddenly came into my consciousness from deep within. I pulled over to the side of the road and asked the Lord to give me a song so that I could quickly remember the words He was speaking to my heart. I titled the Song: *"Rest in Me."* It goes like this:

"Let nothing disturb thee, let nothing make thee afraid. All things are passing, and this too shall pass. I, the Lord your God am in control of your life. I'm at the helm of your ship. Do not be afraid or discouraged, simply rest in me. Simply rest in me."

It reminds me of Psalm 131: 2. "I have stilled my soul like a weaned child to its mother, weaned is my soul" (See Psalm 131:1-3). Another way of saying this verse: "Enough for me to keep my soul tranquil and quiet like a child in its mother's arms." What safety, what protection, what love. And it's free and there for the taking. All we need to do is crawl up into Mama Mary's arms of merciful love or into Jesus's arms and nestle up close to His heart and hear His very heart beat. We have a God in heaven too who is waiting to shower us with His love. His love is safe because it's unconditional. (See Romans 8:15-16; Galatians 4:6-7)

Many people have a hard time trusting God because of hurt, abuse or pain experienced here on earth. I know, because I still struggle with trusting God with my life too. But this is an area in which Satan loves to lie to us. We transfer our faulty thinking onto God and think that His ways are like man's. But they are not. His ways are above our ways and His thoughts are above our thoughts. (See Isaiah 55: 8-9). He is pure, unconditional love and only His love can heal our wounded souls that have been hurt or abused because of others or our own sinful ways. (See John 3:16-18)

1 Peter 5:6-9 tells us: "So humble yourselves under the mighty hand of God, that He may exalt you in due time. Cast all your worries upon Him because He cares for you. Be sober and vigilant. Your opponent the devil is prowling around like a roaring lion looking for someone to devour. Resist him, steadfast in faith, knowing that your fellow believers throughout the world undergo the same sufferings."

He Was There All the Time

Perhaps you have heard the illustration of the frog in a pan of water. If you put a frog in hot water, he will jump out but if you put him in cool water and slowly heat up the water he will not jump out and will eventually die. Sin is just like that. Satan tempts us with little things that eventually get to be bigger things until eventually it kills us. I did little sinful things that turned into bigger sinful things and before I knew it, like the frog, I too was dying emotionally and spiritually. This is exactly how Satan works. He makes sin look so appealing that we want it, never realizing that it will destroy us in the end.

As I grew older and became numb to the sins in my life, it got even easier to sin. Once I opened the door there was no turning back until I repented and asked Jesus and His Mother to help me to face myself honestly and see my need for God to fill the void in my heart. Good Christian people are believing in all kinds of lies, yet God is calling each of us into a life of holiness. I have cried and cried over the lies I believed from saying no to the Lord in the library (when he lovingly asked me to give my heart to Him), to allowing others to take advantage of me when I was young, naïve and vulnerable.

The Bible warns us that we must be wise as serpents and gentle (innocent) as doves (See Matthew 10: 16). While working for the FBI, I worked mostly with married men and I came so close to getting involved with a married man who was in a horrible marriage. He was a "good Catholic man," actively involved in his church, yet looking for love in all the wrong places. I, on the other hand, was an easy prey because I was lonely and longing to be in a loving relationship with someone who loved God and was a devout Catholic. This situation was truly a disaster waiting to happen and I thank the Lord He dissolved that friendship before anything worse took place. Satan lied to me saying it's OK. Once again, the enemy was using our weaknesses to deceive us to sin!

For a brief time, before I married Greg, I lived with a guy on and off. I convinced myself that it was OK because my Catholic pastor said I was not in sin provided we both loved each other and agreed to it. I tried to convince myself that I was going to marry him someday, but that never happened. Many of my friends were living with someone outside of marriage so I too began to convince myself that fornication was OK as well. Satan would say he too is a good Catholic man and everyone is doing it. Lies, lies, lies!

Since returning to the Catholic Church, the Lord has been teaching me that our sexuality is a beautiful gift from God to bring a married couple together in deeper oneness and unity with each other and with God, as well as for the procreation of children. It is not intended to be used or abused as a means of bringing comfort and pleasure to ourselves outside of marriage. The world and society are teaching us that it is OK to have sex outside of marriage provided you are not hurting yourself or others, but this is a lie that many people have fallen into in the past including me! God intended marriage to be a sacred act between one man and one woman and the sexual act is God's way of uniting the couple more deeply. Since coming back to the Catholic Church, I have learned the real meaning of our sexuality, by studying the "Theology of the Body" which is the total self-giving of our souls and bodies to our spouse until death. It's not meant to be a selfish act to satisfy our need for pleasure. But society says if it feels right and two people agree, it's OK. This applies to fornication, adultery, masturbation and homosexual acts. (See Galatians 5:19, Ephesians 5:3, Colossians 3:5-6, Romans 1: 24-28). These acts really hurt God because that is not at all what He intended for our pleasure no matter what any priest, minister or teacher may say! I recall being taught in college that everything is relative. If it feels right to you, then do it. Because I was taught this in a Catholic college, I just thought it must be right and the way I was brought up was just old-fashioned religion. No, it was not old-fashioned religion. It was God's truth versus the lies of Satan! Because of the things I learned in college, I opened the door of my heart to the very dangerous waters of relativism. It's so sad to see so many good people (Christians included) being sucked into these lies of the enemy.

Another subtle lie that many Christians find hard to believe is yoga. I used to love to do yoga for relaxation. I would notice that it put me into a very relaxed and euphoric state. Yet something told me inside (perhaps the Holy Spirit!) that this goes against trusting God to relax me in His way. So again, I went to several priests who told me that there was nothing wrong with it but still I had no peace in my heart. I kept feeling that something was just not right, yet I could not tell myself why. I was in anguish over this for months because I loved the way I felt after doing it! I even did "Christian yoga" hoping to convince myself that it was OK to do. I also talked to some very devout Catholic lay people whom I trusted and who were walking in the Spirit and living very Godly lives. They told me that yoga relates to worship of idols but that it is so subtle, most people don't know or want to believe that it is. I went on the internet to learn more about it and I discovered that they were right! Like me, many people just think it is an exercise that makes you feel good and relaxed. How hard it was to give up, but I finally said OK Lord, thy will be done. I let go of this false idol and once again felt so free in my heart!

Yes, these were just some of the strongholds that the Lord has had to break in me. When under extreme stress, I have turned to food for emotional comfort as well. I have learned that food in moderation is healthy. But at different times in my life, I was using food as a numbing agent to soothe my troubled soul. But all of this was empty, vanity and left me broken and deeply wounded. I had to break the vow and repent of saying no man would tell me what to do, including God! Whenever I would repent of my many sins, Satan would tell me I was still not good enough and how could God ever forgive me and what chance do I ever have of getting to heaven. But Jesus told St. Faustina that the greater the sin the greater the opportunity that person has for God's mercy.

That is my ticket to healing, freedom and peace. It is the ticket for all of us. No matter how bad our sins are, Jesus is there to set us free from all the sins that hold us down.

As I look back on my life I can see how I became the woman I am who was full of fear, worry, doubts of God's goodness and anxiety. It began as a child when I would hear my Dad say we don't have enough money to pay our bills and his favorite saying was "we need to rob Peter to pay Paul." He was always borrowing money from someone. Because of this, I really believed we were going to go broke and I have had to work with the Lord to break this stronghold by telling myself the truth of God's word that God will supply all our needs as I continue to trust Him and lean on Him for wisdom. Dad had two other favorite sayings: "I'll do it my way" and "My way or the highway." I feared the loss of his love and his rejection of me if I didn't do things his way. I feared he would throw me out of his heart and home if I did not obey all his rules. I transferred this fear of Dad onto God. But the Lord, through St. Faustina, is helping me to heal in these areas of my life. I learned to doubt God's goodness because I was always told my dreams were worthless, so I took this to mean I was worthless as well. But the Lord is healing me by telling me His truth that I am fearfully and wonderfully made, and He planted those dreams in my heart (see Psalm 139). The key to my continual healing is to read God's Word daily and believe what He says about me and then put into practice what I am reading.

St. Jerome says to be ignorant of God's Word is to be ignorant of Christ. I know this to be true from my own life's experiences. The more I am coming to know the Lord (in Eucharist and His Word), the more I am getting set free from the lies I believed growing up.

When we bring all our childhood wounds to Jesus, He promises to gently help us and heal us, if we take His medicine which are like daily vitamins for our wounded souls. I am learning from having gotten so sick with the IBS that our thoughts affect our self-talk, which affects our emotions which are in our stomach. To heal my emotions and quiet my stomach, I need to continually change my thought life and the words I speak to myself. I need to believe the truth of what God says about me and not what others say. I need to speak out loud those truths to my heart when Satan tries to remind me of the lies I have believed most of my life. This takes hard work, but it is worth the effort to be truly free! When the sick man came to Jesus and asked Him, "Lord, if you are willing to heal me", the Lord with deep love in His eyes said: "I am willing." I am learning to trust Him to do what I cannot do for myself. I am also learning that He heals in ways I would never expect -- but it's always for my greater good and His highest glory.

This is the Good News that the Lord came to earth to bring to us. What He is doing for me He will do for you too. Just open your heart to Him and pour out all your emotional pain and let His word speak life to you. Let Him break those strongholds that are keeping you from being set free to be the man or woman He has created and destined you to be. For years, I cried out to the Lord to heal me from my physical (IBS) pain "thorn in my flesh" but the Lord has saw fit to let me learn to live with it so that I turn to Him each day for help. This child-like dependency is a greater healing than an actual physical healing. He daily tells me that His grace is sufficient, and His power is made perfect in my weak body (See 2 Corinthians 12:7-10). I literally turn to the Lord and depend on Him for strength, courage and peace, every day, if I want my stomach pain to be kept under control. When I get anxious or upset the pain flairs up but when I turn to the Lord and ask Him to quiet my emotions, my pain quiets down. I am learning how integrated our spirit is to our soul and body. As the Lord says in His word, we truly are fearfully and wonderfully made (See Psalm 139).

The Lord is showing me that my self-talk is a very important part of my healing as well. When a thought comes to my mind, I can either agree with it and speak it to myself or disagree with it. I learned the importance of healthy self-talk while training at Quantico for the FBI. For example, when someone is rude or says something hurtful or sarcastic (which oftentimes hurts me), I can choose to agree with what they said or say to myself this hurtful word or action came from within their heart. So instead of taking it personally, I choose to forgive and pray for them. Our words are powerful to bring life or death to ourselves and each other. (See Proverbs 18:21) The Bible tells us to watch the words that come out of our mouths so that they encourage and build each other up in the faith including ourselves (See James 3:1-12). The Bible also says to always speak the truth in love being patient with each other as well as with ourselves (See Ephesians 4:15). I believed what my Dad said about me, for decades. Because my dreams were worthless to him, I believed I was worthless myself. I know he never meant to incur such pain to his child, but I am learning through this situation that our words need to be carefully chosen before we speak them so that we don't crush one another's spirit or our own. When someone hurts me with their words, I try to look past the words and into their heart and ask the Lord how would you have me to respond (not react to these words). Oftentimes the Lord will tell me that they too are wounded, and those words come from their wounded hearts and that is why I am to pray instead of hurting them in return. When I think of having grown up with a mom who was very negative and depressed most of the time, I now look back and see a very wounded person herself. I can now let go of the anger and hurt I felt and forgive her and ask the Lord to bless her with His love and mercy even though she has since gone home to be with the Lord.

I tell myself that "Father knows best." For most of my life I have either stuffed my emotions or let them rule me which in both cases have been very unhealthy for me and my relationship with others. When I listen to the Lord and let Him father me, I handle life's situations so much better. When I let my emotions rule (like an unruly child) I oftentimes overreact to others or situations and end up with a severe IBS attack. Therefore, I am working on remaining quiet, calm and peaceful in the Lord, taking every thought captive to the obedience to Christ (2 Corinthian 10:5). I cannot control the random steady stream of thoughts that come into my head, but I now ask the Lord is this from you? Is this a truth thought or a lie from the enemy to pull me down and put me back into bondage? The Lord recently showed me something. He told me that when a negative or self-destructive thought comes to me just switch channels as if I was changing the channel on TV. It is that simple -- change from a fleshly thought to a Holy Spirit-filled thought (Philippians 4:4-8).

I am now beginning to understand what that vision was all about, that I had at 18 years old when the Lord said I am going to set you free and as you get set free, you are going to take someone else's hand and they too are going to be set free and so on. I now see that vision being lived out. Will you take my hand and together let us take Jesus' hand and walk out of darkness and lies into His glorious light of mercy, healing, forgiveness and love? He is waiting for us. All we need to do is say yes Lord, here I am! Will you take my empty life and fill it with new wine as you did at the wedding feast of Cana? Mama Mary help us to say yes and to do whatever He asks us to do. Amen.

He Was There All the Time

Growing in Wholeness and Grace

We all battle lust of the flesh, lust of the eyes and pride of life -- the world, the flesh and the devil. That is why we need to be vigilant daily and learn to walk by the Spirit and not our carnal flesh (our impulses, affections and passions) which wants to be in control.

I would like to share some of the things that are helping me to grow in my relationship with the Lord and are helping me to walk more in the Spirit and not my flesh. I have good days and bad, but I know the Lord never leaves my side. He promises to walk with us through thick and thin as we keep running to Him. Pride is our biggest enemy. We must die to ourselves daily and confess our desperate need and dependency on Him for all things. We need to protect ourselves from the subtle and not so subtle lies of the enemy who preys on our needs and weaknesses.

He Was There All the Time

This is like a prescription from the Lord to me and I want to now share it with you. As we take the Lord's medicine, He promises we will become the whole person He destined us to be and fulfill the plans He has for us. What is even more beautiful is that what Satan intended for evil in our lives, the Lord will turn to great good to help others as well (See Romans 8:28). But it takes vulnerability, honesty with ourselves, God and others and deep humility to see ourselves as we really are: sinners in need of a Savior to rescue us and save us from ourselves (our disordered passions, affections), the world and the devil.

The Lord is teaching me to stay away from evil or even the appearance of evil -- to run from it lest I get caught in its web as I have in the past. He is teaching me how to be wise as a serpent yet gentle as a dove. What sometimes appears innocent is evil in disguise, but the Holy Spirit promises to help us with grace to see through the lies and walk in His love and mercy. The Lord does not want me to be naïve or easily misled like I have been in the past.

Here are some of the wonderful ways the Lord is helping me, and I know will help you too. Just choose the ones the Holy Spirit puts on your heart and trust Him to guide and strengthen you through them.

I try to attend Mass daily so that I can become one with my Lord. As I recalled earlier, when I was in Israel, I felt like something was missing in my life. I felt there was more, but I was not sure what that more was until the Lord said to come back to Eucharist. Not only do I sit next to my best friend and share life together by reading His Word, but we become one body and soul in Eucharist -- He in me and me in Him! WOW! It doesn't get any better than that here on earth! All of this takes place in the Holy Sacrifice of the Mass. As a Protestant, we always heard the Word of God preached. Communion was not shared very often and when it was, it was just a memory or formality of the last Supper, not the actual receiving of the real Body, Blood, Soul and Divinity of Jesus Christ. I compare receiving Eucharist like husband and wife becoming intimately one with each other. Nothing can break that bond except sin. When I receive the Lord in Eucharist, He infuses me with His very living presence and power to model Him in my thoughts, words and actions. In other words, He helps me to walk more and more in His Spirit and less and less in my flesh.

Confession/reconciliation is a fabulous way to meet Jesus and pour out my heart to Him and receive not judgment or condemnation but mercy, forgiveness and healing. Best of all, it is free just for the taking!!! A lot of tears have been shed and a lot of healing has occurred in this wonderful well-kept secret place. Jesus says to confess our sins one to another so that we may be healed. When I humble myself before the priest it is really Jesus to whom I am talking. He is just there in proxy for Jesus and something happens when he says: "Your sins are forgiven now go in peace and sin no more." All sin is an offense against God first and against others and ourselves. Such cleansing takes place when we unburden the ills of our hearts to God who loves us so much and wants His very best for our lives! I have died a million deaths in confessing my multitude of sins to the priest, but I have walked out a healthier person, as I gaze upon the cross and see those sins nailed to Jesus who died to take those sins away to give me new life- His life! What liberation. I go as often as I need to go.

Eucharistic Adoration is just heavenly. I love it when I can be alone with my husband; we don't even need to talk; just being together is enough. That is what I think of when I meet my spiritual husband, Jesus, in Holy Adoration. I just want to be with Him and listen to His still small voice tell me He loves me -- I tell Him how much I love Him too. We have had some very open heart to heart talks and much healing has taken place in those quiet moments. I highly recommend it. You will be blessed more than you ever dreamed or imagined! He's a gentleman. He is waiting for you. He stands at the door of our heart and knocks (See Revelation 3:20). All we need to do is open the door of our hearts to the Lord and let Him in to commune with us. It's a wonderful time of intimacy and fellowship between two lovers.

Praying God's Word -- The Bible -- is another way of growing very close to the Lord. There are many wonderful devotionals that can help us deepen our relationship with the Lord, but my favorites are those that contain scriptural readings for daily Mass and morning and evening prayers. I usually look up the passages in my Bible and read the other verses around it to get a clearer picture of what the passage is saying. Then I ask the Lord what is He saying to me as I read this passage. I personalize it and put my name in it and listen carefully for what He is saying. Often, I journal our conversations. St. Faustina kept a journal and I have learned a lot from her. It is a powerful tool to look back on and see where the Lord has brought you. I also like to record prayer requests and answered prayers in my journal as well.

As a Protestant, I learned to read God's word -- the Bible -- carefully, slowly and to meditate on it deeply and contemplatively. We were taught to chew on God's word like a cow chews her cud, repeatedly, until it is very well chewed or deeply understood. We were taught to personalize what we were reading, to hear the Lord speak to our hearts through His word. When I read the Psalms, for example, I will put my name in places and hear the Lord speak to my heart as He did the people in the Old Testament. Do not just read it for head knowledge but for heart knowledge, where our hearts are transformed in the reading of God's word. It's not just a book of nice stories or wise words. It's the very WORD of God Himself and His WORD has the power to change us into His image and make us like Christ and to give us the grace and strength we need to fight the good fight. We need to read it every day to learn how to think like Christ and then, through the strength of the Holy Spirit, (not our own weak strength), put into practice what we just read. A pastor once told me: "God said it, that settles it, I believe it, now I simply and humbly obey," whether it makes sense to my mind or not. I have read many different bibles -- both Catholic and Protestant. I recommend you select a bible that speaks to your heart.

Another practice that is helping me in my faith journey is meditating on the rosary -- not saying it but praying it very, very slowly. When the Lord first called me back to the Catholic Church, He lovingly gave me to His mother, who helped me pray the rosary by meditating on the life of her son, Jesus. To help me deepen this prayerful meditation, I use two different methods. One is a *scriptural* rosary which has a meditation or Bible verse for every Hail Mary bead. The other method uses a CD which gives a summary of each mystery, and I pray the rosary with others on the CD. I feel like I am not alone, and it helps me stay focused because I am easily distracted. I always feel so peaceful when I am done. I feel Mary's presence right there besides me. I know her Son is smiling down upon us as we focus our thoughts on Him; striving to become more like Him through this beautiful meditative prayer.

Another beautiful prayer is the *Chaplet of Divine Mercy* which the Lord taught St. Faustina. When I was thinking about returning to the Catholic Church, the Lord led me to St. Faustina, who took me under her wing and taught me this simple prayer. During my lunch break, I would go off by myself and pray this prayer and such peace would come over me. I did not know at the time that God's graces were coming upon me to get me ready to return to the Catholic faith. Saying the chaplet put a hunger in me for more of the fullness of faith in Him which I have found in the Catholic Church where all treasures lie hidden, waiting to be discovered.

St. Faustina tells us that when we pray the chaplet – especially on behalf of dying persons -- we are asking that God's mercy shield them from God's judgment and wrath for their sins. God never punishes us. We punish ourselves by choosing to sin and not repent. Praying the chaplet for others helps them to choose life over sin and death. It is important to pray it and not just say the words but to truly think about what we are saying. We are thinking about what Jesus did for us on the cross to save us from our sins -- the high price He paid for our salvation and conversion. We also think about how He continues to feed us and heal us through His continual giving of Himself to us in Eucharist. I pray this prayer for all souls, living and dying, especially souls that are at death's door. The Lord told St. Faustina to focus on a picture of His heart with two rays coming out of it, while saying the Divine Mercy Chaplet. The red rays represent His life-giving blood while the pale rays represent the water coming from His blood which washes away our sins. His grace is flowing into us as He is cleansing us of our sins, and filling us with His very life.

Daily I put on the armor of God (Ephesians 6:10-20). He is calling us to be His front men in the daily spiritual battles we all face. The enemy hates anything we do for the Lord, but he cannot do anything that the Lord does not allow him to do; therefore, by fortifying ourselves we will be better prepared for his attacks which oftentimes comes through those whom we love the most! We need to remember that the enemy is not people. He works through people. Therefore, we need to love, forgive, pray and bless others every day.

I like to read stories about the saints who are people just like us who listened and obeyed God no matter the cost. They simply stepped out and "did it afraid." Whatever God asked them to do they just obeyed. We too can become saints as we learn from them and ask their help. After all, we are the mystical body of Christ here to help each other. All we need to do is call upon them and they will help us in our daily struggles to follow Jesus, in His footsteps. They have fought the good fight and won the race. They are great role models.

I also love to listen to Praise and Worship Music because it has a way of elevating my spirit into the presence of God. The Bible tells us to worship the Lord with songs and instruments. This gives glory to His name.

I am learning to be thankful in all circumstances instead of complaining. I might not like the cross I am carrying but I try not to compare my life to others. God will give me the strength I need to follow Him daily as I seek to keep my focus on Him and not others. Job said though the Lord tested him, he chose to trust in Him (Job 13:5). Job also said that the Lord gives life and the Lord takes it away, blessed be the name of the Lord (Job 1:21). The Lord wants me to bless Him, always and in all circumstances. He will see me through if I just trust in Him for wisdom and direction. Romans 8:28 tells us that the Lord works all things out for our good to those that love Him and are called according to His purposes. My favorite life verse is Proverbs 3:5-6: "Trust in the Lord with all your heart, on your own intelligence do not rely; In all your ways be mindful of Him, and He will make straight your paths."

So often I like to just sit in church and meditate on the cross -- this is love. I want His gaze to transform me. I like to meditate on the Stations of the Cross not just during Lent but throughout the year.

He Was There All the Time

We are all called to take up our crosses daily, die to self and live for Him while serving Him and others in humility. Meditating on His passion helps me to keep my focus on Him and not me.

Prayer is simply talking to God from my heart and I love to do this all day long with or without words. I try to bask in His quiet presence in the gift of the eternal now, the gift of the present moment, His Sabbath rest and gaze on Him in solitude. Even if I am busy, I try to talk to Him about everything in the silence of my heart. I ask the Lord to help me let go of the past with its regrets and not dwell there. Also, I ask Him to help me not focus on the future with its cares and fears. He reminds me that He is already there, so I need not worry about tomorrow.

I love reading the *Catechism of the Catholic Church* to learn the truths of our faith and to help me grow in understanding our rich heritage and deposit of faith. I also love to read St. Faustina's diary. She was so real with Jesus. She talked to Him about everything and Jesus loved talking to her as well. It helps me in my own relationship with Jesus to see how they communicated with each other.

I pray to my guardian angel and to St. Michael for protection from the wiles of the enemy. Our heavenly angels and saints are waiting for us to call upon them to help us here on earth. After all, we are the mystical body of Christ. I also pray for our sisters and brothers in purgatory that need our prayers because they cannot pray for themselves. I pray for them especially by offering up my Masses for them, along with praying the rosary and Chaplet of Divine Mercy for them.

I also remind myself that I am never alone. I bought a "commitment ring" to wear to remind me that I am married to the Lord and I never walk alone in this life. He is my first husband and we walk through the day together. I tell myself when upsetting things happen that He already knew this was going to happen and it is for my greater good and the greater good of others and His highest glory. I ask for more childlike trust and confidence in His plans to be fulfilled whether I understand those plans or not. Thy will be done.

When the Lord called me back to the Catholic church I was very nervous about seeking wise counsel from others. I prayed hard for the Holy Spirit to carefully help me choose wise and holy priests with whom to confess my sins. He is so faithful because on each step of my journey, He has sent some very Godly and holy men to help me. On different occasions, when I needed counseling for some emotional or spiritual battle I was struggling with, He again always sent the right person at the right time. The people I have gone to have not only guided me into truth but oftentimes have prayed with me for the Lord's wisdom and help in the difficult situations I was facing. I tend to be very impulsive. When the Lord shows me something that I think is going to happen, I want to immediately go after that thing. I tend to be driven by the "tyranny of the urgent." But through wise counsel, I am learning to wait upon the Lord for HIS timing and not mine. I say to the Lord, if this is truly from you, it will come to pass in your way, means and timing. If it is from me, it will fade away and come to naught. This wise counsel from a very holy priest and spiritual director has brought me great peace. I am not responsible to make things happen. I am simply meant to be the handmaid of the Lord who waits upon Him and does whatever He asks when He says to do it. My job is to simply maintain a quiet, calm, peaceful, patient, prayerful, docile composure so that I can hear the voice of the Lord and be quick to obey His gentle promptings.

It takes hard work because I tend to be a Martha, doer type, rather than Mary at His feet listening first and then doing whatever He tells me. I tend to be more like Martha who does things in my own strength and when I become weary and tired I wonder why am I so fatigued. I ask myself where are you Lord? Why am I so exhausted serving you? It is then I hear Him lovingly say: Come, sit at my feet and I will give you rest. I will refresh you, for my yolk is easy and my burden light when you do it with me and in my way, means and timing rather than doing it in your strength and way." He is teaching me to have a Mary/Martha spirit; not either/or. I am to serve Him with a Mary spirit and not on my own. Once again, I don't always see my own faults and weaknesses clearly. It helps to have an outsider help me see what I don't see and learn from their wise words. When trials come my way, I say: "Jesus, I praise you, Jesus I thank you, Jesus I love you. Jesus, I trust in you. Your will be done in this situation that I am struggling with." I try to remind myself that when things seem dark and I don't see a way out or through, I think to myself a blessing must be coming if I don't give up and get depressed because I don't see answers or a solution. I am learning that it is always darkest before the dawn and oftentimes the Lord comes at the 11th hour! These are the joys of walking by faith in God, His Word, and His promises.

I encourage others to do the same when it comes to picking out confessors or counselors with which to share your heart and soul. Be sure they are walking with the Lord and leading holy, Godly lives. You cannot go wrong. You will grow in holiness and freedom as you discover more and more of God's truth which alone can set you free.

He Was There All the Time

Epilogue

Before we were married, I had told Marvin about my encounter with St. Faustina while working in the Protestant ministry in Missouri. I shared with him how she had helped me return to Holy Eucharist and the Catholic Church. He also shared with me his encounter with the Blessed Mother and Jesus while he was on a pilgrimage to Poland two years after the death of his wife. He had gone to Poland seeking answers from the Lord as to what to do with his life. While at the Shrine of Our Lady of Czestochowa, Our Lady spoke to him, telling him to do whatever Her son tells him to do. The following day, on the feast of St. Thomas, the Apostle, the Lord told him to "stop unbelieving and believe." While he was seeking answers for his future in Poland, I was seeking answers from the Lord in Israel. Little did we ever dream that the Lord was going to join us together for a future ministry serving Him.

While in Krakow, Marvin and his fellow pilgrims visited the Wawel Cathedral and climbed the tower containing the Sigismund Bell.

He Was There All the Time

Marvin was told by the tour guide that if he touched the bell's clapper before the bell rang at noon, the next time he would return to Krakow, he would be accompanied by his bride. He was not thinking about marriage – he was not even dating at the time – but he struck the clapper anyway.

That is why it was so fitting that Marvin and I celebrate our 5th wedding anniversary while on a pilgrimage to Poland in June 2017. The pilgrimage was entitled: *In the Footsteps of St. John Paul II and Saint Faustina* and we truly had the opportunity to walk in the footsteps of those two most glorious saints. Even more so, before Marvin and I were married, I told him how much St. Faustina had meant to me and how God used her and our Blessed Mother to bring me home to the rich fullness of the Catholic Church. I could think of no better way to celebrate our anniversary.

After a few days in Warsaw, we traveled to Swinice, Warckie and visited the home where St. Faustina – Helena Kowalska – was born and raised – a two room house where she lived with her parents and her nine siblings. We also visited her parish Church – St. Casimir's -- where she was baptized, made her first confession, and received her first communion and where her family attended weekly Mass. We drove down the long road that St. Faustina used to walk to get to the church and it was not easy especially on those very cold winter days!

St. Faustina had an incredible child-like faith and she trusted Jesus and Mary for everything. When the Lord called her to leave her rural home, she boarded a train and went to Warsaw, not knowing where to go or what to do when she arrived there. We saw the train station that she disembarked. Once there, she asked the Lord and His Mother what to do next. They literally led her to a place to stay and to a nearby church to talk to a priest. We visited that church. What faith, what trust, what surrender-- To be all alone with no one, but the Lord, to lead, guide and direct her every step! Her life journey reminded me of my own and how the Lord has asked me too to walk by faith, with child-like trust and confidence, totally trusting in Him when nothing makes sense.

We later visited – not once but twice – the Shrine of Divine Mercy in Lagiewnicki, just outside of Krakow. It was in the convent here where the Lord appeared to St. Faustina and spoke to her and where she wrote her famous diary. We saw her convent and chapel where she lies in rest. I felt like we were walking on holy ground. In fact, IT WAS HOLY GROUND!!! I could literally feel the presence of the Lord as we sat in her little chapel and prayed the Divine Mercy chaplet with the sisters. We had extended our stay in Poland by a day so that we would have additional time to spend at the Shrine. It was well worth the time and the cost!!!

The sweet sister who was our tour guide took us to a building that housed a re-creation of Sister Faustina's bedroom. It was a very

He Was There All the Time

simple humble room just like her. But what affected me most was the story she shared. Sister said that there used to be a gate where the building now stands. When Sister Faustina became very sick, she was given the task of gatekeeper. One cold, day, a very poor, starving, tattered-clothed beggar came to the gate. He asked for food. Sister Faustina immediately went to the kitchen and found him some soup and bread, which he ate up immediately. He then told her that He was Jesus and that He was pleased with the way she treated Him and the poor people who came to her gate. He then disappeared! We were standing on the very spot where Jesus appeared to her! Again, I felt like this very spot was holy ground. I also felt the Lord speak to my heart that He was asking the same of me. I never know who He is going to send my way, but I am to show love and mercy to the souls He sends, no matter their poverty (physical, spiritual, emotional, financial). I felt that he was calling me to be the gatekeeper to His church and to invite people in, to be fed and healed. The Lord showed me that His church is a hospital where He (Dr. Jesus) and Nurse Mary are waiting to heal people.

Prior to our pilgrimage to the Divine Mercy Shrine, we had visited St. John Paul II's birthplace and childhood home in Wadowice – it is now a beautiful museum – where he lived with his parents and older brother which is located right next door to the church where he – Karol Wojtyla -- was baptized – the baptismal fount is still there -- and received the sacraments of Reconciliation and Eucharist.

The story that touched my heart the most was that of his mother's death and the effect it had on him. At the tender age of 9, his mother died, and his father immediately took him to the church and said, as they stood in front of the Blessed Mother's statue: "This is your Mother, now. She will take care of you." We saw the beautiful statue of Mary that he stood in front of as he dedicated his life to her, in child-like trust. St. John Paul II had a real intimate and personal relationship with the Blessed Mother, just like St. Faustina. He really trusted her with everything!

As I thought about this story, I thought of my own life again. When I was in Israel, the Lord led me to Mount Carmel to His Mother and it was there that I lit the candle and asked her to help me too. Little did I know how powerful she would be to help me return to the Catholic Church and to a deeper more intimate relationship with her Son! The guide at the museum told us the story of when St. John Paul II was nearly assassinated in the Vatican. His faith in "His Mother" was so strong, he said one hand fired the bullet, but another guided it. He felt that the Blessed Mother saved his life. In thanksgiving, he visited Lourdes after recovery and placed the bullet in Our Lady's crown. He also paid a visit to the man who tried to kill him and forgave him. What mercy! What love! This message spoke to my heart about the importance of forgiveness in my own life and how healing it is to simply forgive everyone, everything and leave the consequences to God.

Later in our pilgrimage, we walked the streets of Krakow where St. John Paul II studied at the Jagiellonian University, was ordained to the priesthood, and later served as Cardinal Archbishop before his election to the papacy. We celebrated Mass at the St. John Paull II Center & Sanctuary right next door to the Shrine of Divine Mercy in Lagiewnicki. Still under construction, it was dedicated just prior to World Youth Day in 2016. It also is the burial site of St. John Paul II.

While on pilgrimage in Poland, we also walked in the footsteps of St. Maximilian Kolbe, from the monastery he established in Niepokalanow where we celebrated Mass that day, to his death cell in the Nazi concentration camp, Auschwitz, where we celebrated his life and death.

Our visit to Auschwitz affected me in two ways. We were told the story of how St. Maximillian Kolbe willingly laid down his life to save that of another prisoner. We saw the cell in which he died and heard about the horrible torture he endured. But instead of being bitter, he too forgave, and he humbly lived Christ in word and deed before the other prisoners in his tiny cell. Ten men were placed in this tiny cell to die of starvation. Some of the men went insane but he prayed for the other men who were with him. His faith kept him strong in the most horrific situations that he was put through. After all the other men died, he was still alive and after two weeks, the Nazis injected him with poison and killed him.

Again, the Lord spoke to my heart about loving and forgiving my enemies (or anyone who hurts me for that matter) and the importance of reflecting Jesus in my thoughts, words and deeds every day, no matter how difficult my circumstances. I also learned the importance of being patient with others who are struggling in their difficult situations. These men did not have the faith of St. Maximillian Kolbe, but in love, He reflected the love and mercy of Jesus, expecting nothing in return from them. His needs -- for strength and courage during severe suffering – were met through Jesus and His Blessed Mother, with whom he too was very close. Like St. John Paul and St. Faustina, he too had a very deep and intimate relationship with Jesus and Mary. There is no way he could have endured what he went through without their help! I learned they are there for me too, if I just rely on them as he did! Again, what child-like faith!!!

While at Auschwitz, we also learned about Doctor Joseph Mengele, a physician who performed deadly human experiments on prisoners, most tragically and horrifically on twin children. He would put them through excruciatingly painful experiments and then watch them die. Our guide told us about one set of twin girls, age ten who suffered severe abuse at the hands of this doctor.

He Was There All the Time

Young, innocent lives were tortured because of hate. I left Auschwitz feeling such sadness and sickness of heart. But God did not leave me there in my pain. An incredible thing happened the very next day.

While eating breakfast at our hotel, someone from our tour group, came over to our table and told us that one of the twins that we had just heard about in our tour of Auschwitz was there eating breakfast. She was now in her 80's and living in Indiana. She had brought a tour group to Auschwitz to share her story! But what she was sharing was not what we expected to hear. She told her companions that she was here to teach them about forgiveness. Her sister eventually died due to kidney failure because of the horrible experiments done to her as a child. But she went through a very unexpected inner healing wherein she went back to Germany many years later and forgave one of Mengele's assistants, who was there when Mengele abused her and her sister. We learned that this "twin" brings groups to Auschwitz to tell them that if you want healing it begins with total and complete forgiveness. Knowing a little of what she went through and seeing her sit there left me in awe. This was a divine appointment. How powerful forgiveness, mercy and healing are if we let the Lord do His surgery on our wounded souls! We just need to have the courage to come home to His Church/hospital to receive His healing touch.

A beautiful thing happened while visiting Our Lady's shrine at Czestochowa. As I noted above, Marvin had visited the shrine previously and it was there where Our Lady spoke to him. We asked our spiritual director if we could renew our wedding vows there, as we would be celebrating our 5th wedding anniversary on the very day we were in Czestochowa. And we did!! Again, a divine appointment, perfect timing. It was a beautiful moment for both of us. That evening in Krakow, we were scheduled to have dinner at a restaurant called "The Reception" – as in "wedding reception". Our tour guide did not know that we were renewing out vows earlier in the day, but upon discovering this, he decided to call the restaurant and plan a traditional Polish wedding reception, with real salt, real vodka and real Polish mountain music and dancing! It was a most memorable evening!!

I would like to conclude this memoir by sharing a parable I once heard. Picture yourself walking along the sandy ocean beach and you see a starfish that has been washed ashore. That starfish cannot put himself in the water yet if he doesn't get back into the water, he will die. He needs to be picked up and thrown back in. He helplessly looks up at you to help him. Despite his prickles, you carefully pick him up and put him in the water where he will thrive. As he swims away, you know you were placed there at such a time as this, to help this creature and you smile as you walk on, knowing that this was a divine appointment orchestrated by the Lord.

As I reflect on our pilgrimage to Poland I see that our lives are like this: Every day, the Lord sends people onto our path who need His ocean of love, forgiveness and mercy. They are wounded and hurting, and they are just waiting for someone to love them and place them into the arms of the Lord who will heal them. Will we – you and I -- be that person?

I also see that poor beggar man standing at the gate. Perhaps that person is you. I see me in that poor, broken person, and I see how the Lord sent St. Faustina and His Mother to feed and help me to heal by bringing me home to His Church. Now the Lord is asking me to be His gatekeeper and invite others to His church/hospital where He can feed and heal their tattered wounds.

When I think of St. Maximillian Kolbe and the woman who was severely abused at Auschwitz so humbly forgiving their enemies, I see that it is possible to love, forgive, pray and bless others and thus walk in Jesus's footsteps. The doors of His church are open: doors of love, healing, forgiveness and mercy. Will you walk through them? He is waiting to heal and set you free. And as you get healed, will you take someone else's hand and bring them home too?

There are many starfish waiting, and poor broken souls waiting to be carried into their Father's arms of love. The Lord is calling you and me. Come home, my child, come home. St. Augustine says, "You have made us for yourself, O Lord, and our hearts are restless until they rest in You." Jesus says that you shall know the truth and the truth will set you free. He is the truth and if we surrender our hearts and lives to Him and His will daily, we will truly be free (John 8:32). Be healed. Just get out of the boat and walk on water with Jesus. He promises to hold you up; and if need be: "Just do it Afraid!" No regrets; only blessings. To God be all glory! Amen!

He Was There All the Time

Acknowledgements

I want to thank the Lord and His Mother, along with St. Faustina for bringing me back to the Catholic faith.

I want to thank my beloved husband, Marvin, for his continual encouragement, love, faithfulness and devotion to me while I struggled through many difficult trials these past few years. He kept telling me you have a story to share and you need to write it. So often I have wanted to give up, but he kept saying "write on." I can't thank Him enough. He truly is a gift from God to me.

Also, I want to acknowledge my precious deceased, husband, Greg, who suffered so much while he was alive. His example of humility, faithfulness and love despite severe suffering has given me the strength to keep my eyes fixed on Jesus and take up my cross daily and follow Him no matter the cost.

For my two, wonderful Divine Mercy Cenacles, my "Monday Morning" prayer group, and Christian Women in Action (CWIA). I could not be where I am today if it were not for their support and example of living Godly lives.

Lastly, I want to thank all the souls who will read this story and see the hand of God working in their lives as well. May they find hope, healing and courage to get out of the boat and "Do It Afraid." Just do whatever He is asking you to do. Praise the Lord! Amen

Made in the USA
Middletown, DE
19 May 2018